S. Hrg. 113–461

COMBATING FORCED LABOR AND MODERN-DAY SLAVERY IN EAST ASIA AND THE PACIFIC

HEARING

BEFORE THE

SUBCOMMITTEE ON EAST ASIAN AND PACIFIC AFFAIRS

OF THE

COMMITTEE ON FOREIGN RELATIONS
UNITED STATES SENATE

ONE HUNDRED THIRTEENTH CONGRESS

SECOND SESSION

JULY 8, 2014

Printed for the use of the Committee on Foreign Relations

Available via the World Wide Web: http://www.gpo.gov/fdsys/

U.S. GOVERNMENT PRINTING OFFICE

91–141 PDF   WASHINGTON : 2014

For sale by the Superintendent of Documents, U.S. Government Printing Office
Internet: bookstore.gpo.gov   Phone: toll free (866) 512–1800; DC area (202) 512–1800
Fax: (202) 512–2104   Mail: Stop IDCC, Washington, DC 20402–0001

COMMITTEE ON FOREIGN RELATIONS

ROBERT MENENDEZ, New Jersey, *Chairman*

BARBARA BOXER, California
BENJAMIN L. CARDIN, Maryland
JEANNE SHAHEEN, New Hampshire
CHRISTOPHER A. COONS, Delaware
RICHARD J. DURBIN, Illinois
TOM UDALL, New Mexico
CHRISTOPHER MURPHY, Connecticut
TIM KAINE, Virginia
EDWARD J. MARKEY, Massachusetts

BOB CORKER, Tennessee
JAMES E. RISCH, Idaho
MARCO RUBIO, Florida
RON JOHNSON, Wisconsin
JEFF FLAKE, Arizona
JOHN McCAIN, Arizona
JOHN BARRASSO, Wyoming
RAND PAUL, Kentucky

DANIEL E. O'BRIEN, *Staff Director*
LESTER E. MUNSON III, *Republican Staff Director*

SUBCOMMITTEE ON EAST ASIAN AND PACIFIC AFFAIRS

BENJAMIN L. CARDIN, Maryland, *Chairman*

CHRISTOPHER MURPHY, Connecticut
BARBARA BOXER, California
TOM UDALL, New Mexico
EDWARD J. MARKEY, Massachusetts

MARCO RUBIO, Florida
RON JOHNSON, Wisconsin
JEFF FLAKE, Arizona
JOHN McCAIN, Arizona

(II)

CONTENTS

COMBATING FORCED LABOR AND MODERN–DAY SLAVERY IN EAST ASIA AND THE PACIFIC

TUESDAY, JULY 8, 2014

U.S. SENATE,
SUBCOMMITTEE ON EAST ASIAN AND PACIFIC AFFAIRS,
COMMITTEE ON FOREIGN RELATIONS,
Washington, DC.

The subcommittee met, pursuant to notice, at 10:30 a.m., in room SD–419, Dirksen Senate Office Building, Hon. Benjamin L. Cardin (chairman of the subcommittee) presiding.

Present: Senators Cardin and Rubio.

OPENING STATEMENT OF HON. BENJAMIN L. CARDIN, U.S. SENATOR FROM MARYLAND

Senator CARDIN. Well, good morning and welcome to the Subcommittee on East Asia and the Pacific for today's hearing.

Senator Rubio has indicated to me that he will be here shortly, but that it is certainly okay for us to start the hearing. And I want to give a maximum amount of time for the committee to have a discussion.

Slavery still exists. It exists around the world today, and it is something that we cannot allow to continue. Trafficking is the modern-day slavery. We understand that. And, thanks to the U.S. leadership, we have taken action not only in the United States, but we have been a global leader in combating modern-day slavery and trafficking.

I am proud of the role that the U.S. Helsinki Commission has played. I had the honor this year to chair the U.S. Helsinki Commission. It rotates between the House and the Senate. My cochairman, Chris Smith, has been one of the leaders on trafficking issues.

But, going back many years ago, the Helsinki Commission raised the issue of trafficking as a human rights issue and discussed the matter in which the United States could play a major role. As a result of the hearings in our Commission, the OSCE took major steps to help all 57 states in the OSCE deal with trafficking issues. But, it also led to the passage of the Victims of Trafficking and Violence Protection Act in 2000, and we now have what is known as the Trafficking in Persons Report that we receive every year. This report, to me, is extremely valuable. And whenever an Ambassador from another country or a leader from another country is in my office, I look at this report, and it becomes part of the conversation as to what they are doing in regards to addressing trafficking.

In 2010, we added the United States as one of the countries that we evaluate, because no country is perfect, and every country can improve. The Trafficking in Persons Report has four categories in which countries are listed: Tier 1, which is those countries that are in basic compliance with international standards to combat trafficking; Tier 2 are countries that are not there yet, but we believe are on the right path toward accomplishing and meeting their international responsibilities; Tier 2 Watch List, which are countries that are not moving in the right direction—they have made some progress, but they must do more to comply with their international responsibilities; and Tier 3, those countries that are out of compliance. If a country is in the Tier 2 Watch List for 2 consecutive years, there is a requirement they be downgraded to Tier 3 unless a waiver is sought, which can last for only up to 2 years. If a country is in Tier 3, the consequences can be possible foreign aid restrictions. So, it is an important guide for us to determine what to do.

Now, trafficking can take many forms. We all know about young girls and boys that are trafficked for prostitution. That is a matter that should be of outrage to everyone. But, we also traffic labor, which should also be outrageous to everyone.

So, today's hearing is combating forced labor and modern-day slavery in East Asia and the Pacific. And, for those who have been following the hearings of the subcommittee, you know we have had many hearings dealing with the Rebalance to Asia. We have looked at it from many different points of view. We have looked at it from human rights and good governance, we have looked at it from the economic point of view, we have looked at it from the military security point of view. And our objective has been to strengthen the bilateral ties between the countries of East Asia and the Pacific and the United States, consistent with President Obama's policies. But, our bilateral relationship is very much dependent upon the fundamental human rights, rule of law, and the dignity for vulnerable women, men, and children, and the commitments made by the countries of East Asia and the Pacific.

The International Labor Organization has come out with some startling numbers. One-third of the global illegal profits generated from the use of forced labor in the private sector are made in Asia and the Pacific. Illegal profits obtained through the use of forced labor in the private economy worldwide are estimated to be about $150 billion per year. Over one-third comes from the Asia-Pacific region. It is a problem that we need to focus on. Of the 20.9 million forced labor victims worldwide, 11.7 million, more than half, are estimated to be in the Asia-Pacific region. That is why we are holding this hearing. We are holding this hearing to get a better understanding of what can be done in regards to forced labor trafficking.

And let me point out, we are all consumers, and in many cases, we are buying products that have been produced, in part, by forced labor. But we can be better in helping solve this problem of forced labor and modern-day slavery.

The TIP Report that I referred to had some disappointing downgrades of countries that are within the jurisdiction of this subcommittee. Thailand, a long-time ally of the United States, has been downgraded. And Malaysia, which is a TPP-aspirant country, has also been downgraded. We have several countries that are on the Tier 2 Watch List: Brunei, Cambodia, Laos, Marshall Islands, Solomon Islands, and Timor-Leste. These are countries that we expect better from, particularly if they are to achieve a stronger bilateral relationship with the United States.

So, one positive sign, I might point out, is that China, which was previously Tier 3, is now on Tier 2 Watch List. That is an improvement, and we hope that those improvements will continue. And I expect it had something to do with the fact that they have eliminated their—or at least have made a commitment to eliminate their reeducation through labor provisions.

So, today we have a panel of experts with us who can help us sort out where we are on forced labor and the trafficking. And I am pleased to introduce our witnesses that are on the first panel.

Scot Marciel, who has been a frequent visitor to this committee—we thank you for your participation—the Principal Deputy Assistant Secretary for the Bureau of East Asia and Pacific Affairs at the State Department, a career member of the Senior Foreign Service, previously served as U.S. Ambassador to the Republic of Indonesia.

And he is joined by Lou CdeBaca, the Ambassador at Large for the Office to Monitor and Combat Trafficking in Persons, served as Ambassador at Large and Senior Advisor to the Secretary, and directs the State Department's Office to Monitor and Combat Trafficking in Person, previously served as counsel to the House Committee on Judiciary, and one of our country's most decorated Federal prosecutors at the Department of Justice.

So, we have two people who I think can help us greatly understand this. As I think both of you understand, as is the practice of our committee, your formal written statement, without objection, will be included in the committee record, as will the second panel's formal statements, without objection.

So, Scot, you may proceed as you wish.

STATEMENT OF HON. SCOT MARCIEL, PRINCIPAL DEPUTY ASSISTANT SECRETARY FOR EAST ASIAN AND PACIFIC AFFAIRS, U.S. DEPARTMENT OF STATE, WASHINGTON, DC

Ambassador MARCIEL. Thank you. Chairman Cardin, members of the subcommittee, thank you for the opportunity to testify today on human trafficking in the Asia-Pacific region.

It is really a privilege for me to be able to testify alongside Ambassador CdeBaca. He and his team, as you have mentioned, have done so much to combat trafficking across the region and around the world.

I have worked on human trafficking issues both here in Washington and abroad, most recently as Ambassador to Indonesia. There, among many other anti-trafficking activities that we did, I was involved, for example, in the MTV End Exploitation and Trafficking Campaign in 2012. This is an effort that U.S. Government has funded. It has been very successful in raising awareness about the dangers of trafficking in Southeast Asia.

Human trafficking, as you mentioned, Mr. Chairman, remains a visible and pressing concern in East Asia and the Pacific. While governments across the region are more aware of the issue than in years past, and many are doing more to combat it, progress to date is insufficient. Many governments in the region have developed legal and policy frameworks to deal with trafficking, and several have recently enacted comprehensive anti-trafficking laws. However, implementation of these laws is sometimes weak.

And the insufficient progress on anti-trafficking efforts is sometimes linked to broader challenges facing some of these governments: inadequate rule of law, a weak justice system, and corruption. So, the State Department seeks to sustain progress on these issues, because they are key to development and to democracy and, of course, to more effective efforts against trafficking.

So, the EAP Bureau and—along with our colleagues from the JTIP office, work closely with foreign governments and international partners on strategies and programs to prevent trafficking, protect victims in vulnerable populations, and prosecute offenders. And, in this, the TIP Report is actually a very effective tool, as you mentioned, Mr. Chairman.

In his letter accompanying this year's report, Secretary Kerry stated that, ''We face no greater assault on basic freedom than the evil of human trafficking.'' And in EAP, Assistant Secretary Danny Russell and I and our Ambassadors throughout the region regularly meet and encourage governments to do more against trafficking. We use the TIP Report and other tools, working throughout Asia, to increase public awareness, encourage better and more effective legislation, and promote greater efforts to prevent trafficking, investigate and prosecute trafficking crimes, and assist victims.

Because so much of the work that we do is done by our embassies, I would like to highlight a few examples of some of the work that our embassies in the field have been doing.

For example, our Embassy in Cambodia recently hosted the first-ever Anti-Trafficking Tech Camp, where technologists and civil society organizations, together, developed creative, low-cost, easy-to-use solutions for areas with historically high rates of trafficking. Our Embassy staff in Cambodia also worked with the Ministry of Labor there to develop an interactive voice-response system that makes information on safe migration readily available by phone throughout the country. The Embassy is also working with Cambodian authorities to develop policies and guidelines for conducting undercover investigations of human trafficking.

Our Embassy in Thailand is supporting NGOs that help migrants and trafficking victims get access to justice. Our programs are enhancing Thai investigation and prosecution capacity, and we are arranging to place a technical advisor in the Ministry of Labor to help guide policies on forced labor trafficking.

In the Pacific Islands, our Embassies are encouraging greater effort to tackle forced labor on fishing vessels. In the Marshall Islands, we are providing technical assistance in support of the government's drafting of anti-trafficking legislation and working to help the police and prosecutors understand how better to identify and prosecute trafficking crimes.

In all of our Embassies, our Ambassadors and our Embassy staff regularly engage with host government officials, civil society, and international partners to highlight the importance of increased anti-trafficking efforts. I can say, from my own experience, that this effort is well integrated into our Embassies' overall plans, as well as its daily work.

Finally, in addition to bilateral efforts, we are acting at the regional level. With the TIP office funding, we supported the first-ever ASEAN–United States Joint Regional Project to Combat Human Trafficking and the American Bar Association's Rule of Law Initiative to train heads of anti-traffic units from all 10 ASEAN countries.

Looking forward, we are committed to continuing our work with governments throughout the Asia-Pacific region to help them more effectively combat human trafficking. EAP and the TIP office will continue to work closely together to assess the situation, develop programs and diplomatic strategies to better combat trafficking, and encourage governments to take action to prevent trafficking, protect victims, and prosecute traffickers.

Mr. Chairman, thank you again for the opportunity to testify today. I look forward to your questions.

Thank you.

[The prepared statement of Ambassador Marciel follows:]

PREPARED STATEMENT AMBASSADOR SCOT MARCIEL

INTRODUCTION

Chairman Cardin, Ranking Member Rubio, members of the subcommittee, thank you for the opportunity to testify today on human trafficking in the Asia-Pacific region. It is a privilege to stand alongside my colleague, Ambassador CdeBaca, whose experience and expertise help us boost anti-trafficking efforts across the Asian-Pacific region.

I would also like to thank the subcommittee for its contributions to combating human trafficking, and to thank you, in particular, Mr. Chairman, for your leadership on this issue.

TRAFFICKING IN ASIA-PACIFIC

Human trafficking remains a visible and pressing concern in East Asia and the Pacific. While governments across the region have an increased awareness of trafficking in persons, corruption and a lack of political commitment hinder more substantial gains in some countries. Many governments in the Asia-Pacific have developed adequate legal and policy frameworks to deal with human trafficking, and several have recently enacted laws that comprehensively combat this crime; however, implementation of these trafficking laws is sometimes weak. It is important to note that, in some countries, the limited progress we have seen on anti-trafficking efforts is linked to a broader set of challenges facing the government. When civilians routinely encounter police intimidation, corrupt judges, or poorly trained immigration officials, human rights violations go unnoticed, unaccounted for, and multiply. In countries where this occurs, State Department officials seek sustained adherence to rule of law, democratic practices, and good governance. Expanding democracy and respect for human rights is central to our policy in Asia-Pacific, and combating human trafficking is a priority for the Bureau domestically and at our embassies abroad.

The East Asian and Pacific Affairs (EAP) Bureau collaborates closely with the Department's Office to Monitor and Combat Trafficking in Persons (the TIP Office) not only to draft and publish the ''Trafficking in Persons (TIP) Report,'' but to work throughout the year on strategies and programs aimed at preventing trafficking, protecting victims and vulnerable populations, and prosecuting offenders. In Washington and in our embassies, EAP and the TIP Office regularly share updates, lessons learned, and expertise to secure on-the-ground ''buy-in'' from governments, civil society organizations, and international partners to effectively combat trafficking in persons. We place a huge emphasis on working together to encourage foreign governments to improve their anti-trafficking responses.

As mentioned in this year's TIP Report, simply equating human trafficking to sexual exploitation misses much of the story. Labor trafficking, prevalent throughout the region, is also a crime against human dignity and human security. Worldwide the majority of trafficking victims are held in labor trafficking situations, though we know sexual exploitation often occurs with labor trafficking as well.

The EAP Bureau understands the importance of addressing all forms of trafficking and, with the TIP Office's support, has strongly encouraged governments to do the same. As a direct result of the annual TIP Report and sustained U.S. engagement, some foreign government officials no longer ask for the definition of trafficking or for proof that it exists within their respective borders. Rather, many officials are now asking what steps they can take to improve their anti-trafficking efforts. In short, the TIP Report has facilitated substantive discussions abroad to strengthen political will, to draft and implement TIP legislation, and to further increase public awareness on the issue.

Because so much of this important work is done by our embassies, in the next few minutes I would like to highlight a few examples over the past year where U.S. embassies in the region have worked with host governments and civil society to combat trafficking. Our work in the region is vital, not only because it increases awareness of and local capacity to address TIP, but also because, in private and public engagements, we persistently stress to host governments the importance of increased action and attention to sex and labor trafficking.

Our Embassy in Cambodia remains active in boosting anti-trafficking efforts in cooperation with the government and has recently hosted the first ever anti-trafficking TechCamp where technologists and civil society organizations developed creative, low-cost, and easy-to-use solutions for areas with historically high rates of trafficking. Ambassador Todd not only personally invited Cambodian youth to volunteer throughout the TechCamp, but also publicized the success of the local event on his official blog.

Additionally, Embassy staff worked with the Cambodian Ministry of Labor to develop an interactive voice response system, which makes information on safe migration more readily available by phone throughout the country. In the area of victim protection, we have helped over 760 victims in the past year and will continue to support services to trafficking survivors, including repatriation, medical care, psychosocial support, reintegration, and legal aid. To improve efforts to prosecute trafficking crimes, we are working with the Ministry of Justice to develop policies and guidelines for conducting undercover investigations of human trafficking.

In China, Department officials continue to encourage the Chinese Government to improve efforts to prosecute trafficking offenses and protect victims, make legal reforms to prohibit all forms of trafficking, end forced labor in state-sponsored detention centers, and transparently share information on its anti-trafficking efforts. Embassy Beijing continues to advance the U.S. Government's anti-trafficking agenda with counterparts within the Chinese Ministry of Foreign Affairs and PRC law enforcement ministries; and by actively recruiting up-and-coming Chinese officials to participate in International Visitor Leadership Programs (IVLPs) and other capacity-building programs.

Since FY 2012, we have sent six professionals from Malaysia to the United States on TIP-focused exchange programs (International Visitor Leadership Program) and plan to send another four in FY 2015. In our diplomatic engagements, we regularly and strongly urge Malaysian officials to improve treatment of trafficking victims by reforming its current victim protection regime.

In the Pacific Islands, we encourage additional efforts to address forced labor on fishing vessels in the Pacific and other forms of trafficking. The U.S. Ambassador and his staff supported the Republic of the Marshall Islands (RMI) Attorney General's Office's request for technical assistance and legal advice for the TIP Task Force as it writes the RMI's TIP legislation. The Embassy reached out to the TIP Office to request short-term training and technical assistance; the request was approved by Ambassador CdeBaca, and the TIP Office plans to provide assistance in the coming year. Planned technical assistance includes a component for police and prosecutors on how to identify and prosecute TIP using the laws proposed. Partnerships like these, where we provide some support and guidance to governments with a significant stake in positive outcomes, will bring long-term success.

As Ambassador CdeBaca notes in his testimony, Thailand made a concerted effort over the past year to improve its anti-trafficking data collection and continued to prosecute and convict traffickers. Despite this progress, the government did not make sufficient efforts to address forced labor among foreign migrant workers—including in the fishing industry—and to address reported official complicity in human trafficking.

Embassy Bangkok will continue to support NGOs that help provide access to justice for migrants and trafficking victims. Department staff will also continue to work to enhance Thai capacity to investigate trafficking cases and prosecute perpetrators by training law enforcement officers at our International Law Enforce-

ment Academy (ILEA) in Bangkok and by arranging other police-to-police cooperation and networking with counterparts along the Thai border. Embassy Bangkok
will also arrange the placement of a technical advisor in the Ministry of Labor to
help guide policies on forced labor trafficking.

In Thailand and elsewhere, our ambassadors and embassy staff engage regularly
with host government officials, local civil society organizations, and international
partners to stress the importance of increasing efforts to combat sex and labor traf-
ficking.I would like to reiterate how important it is ensure that both local politicians
and local civil society leaders are taking ownership of the TIP problem in their respective countries. For example, with continued U.S. Embassy support on TIP, the
New Zealand government has partnered with the Salvation Army to identify and
educate vulnerable populations in specific communities on the dangers and charac-
teristics of forced labor.

Lastly, I would like to highlight our regional TIP efforts. With U.S. encourage-
ment, the Association of Southeast Asian Nations (ASEAN) held its 6th Expert
Group Meeting on Trafficking in Persons last month. The group is working to create
a regional plan of action and hold a workshop on human trafficking later this year.
With the TIP Office funding, the State Department supported what became the first-
ever ASEAN-United States joint regional project to combat human trafficking,
fulfilling a Presidential commitment from November 2012.

The TIP Office issued a grant to the American Bar Association's Rule of Law Initiative to train heads of specialized anti-trafficking units from all 10 ASEAN member countries with ASEAN Secretariat support and enhance cross-border collaboration to combat human trafficking.

With U.S. Government funding, the MTV End Exploitation and Trafficking
(MTV–EXIT) campaign has raised a tremendous amount of TIP awareness in Southeast Asia, particularly with the youth demographic. In Indonesia, I personally witnessed how an MTV–EXIT campaign in West Java in September 2012 raised public
awareness by engaging with literally tens of thousands of people, influential local
leaders and politicians, and millions more via live broadcast on TV. Additionally, in
January 2013, MTV–EXIT made roadshows and youth engagement activities in several cities in Indonesia such as in Pontianak (West Kalimantan), Lombok (West
Nusa Tenggara), and Sukabumi (West Java). Education on human trafficking is
especially important to facilitating change in this region, where trafficking is so
widespread. This program has been extremely successful and an important part of
our successes in Southeast Asia.

CONCLUSION

As we look toward the future, our Bureau and embassies and consulates in the
EAP region are committed to working with foreign governments to help them more
effectively combat human trafficking. EAP and the TIP Office will continue to col-
laborate to assess the situation; develop programs and diplomatic strategies to better combat trafficking; and encourage governments to take action to prevent trafficking, protect victims, and prosecute traffickers.

Mr. Chairman, I thank you for the opportunity to appear before you today to discuss human trafficking in Asia-Pacific. I look forward to answering any questions
the subcommittee may have.

Senator CARDIN. Thank you, Secretary Marciel.
Ambassador CdeBaca.

STATEMENT OF LUIS CdeBaca, AMBASSADOR AT LARGE FOR THE OFFICE TO MONITOR AND COMBAT TRAFFICKING IN PERSONS, U.S. DEPARTMENT OF STATE, WASHINGTON, DC

Ambassador CdeBaca. Thank you, Chairman Cardin, for the
opportunity to speak with you today.

And I—just a note of personal privilege—Scot Marciel, not only
with the MTV Exit Program, but also in his time both within EAP
and at post, has been a real leader on this. I just wish that we had
a photo of him at that MTV concert out on the stage to offer for
the record. [Laughter.]

A few weeks ago, the Secretary of State released the 14th Annual
Trafficking in Persons Report, what Secretary Kerry called a
"Roadmap for the Journey to Freedom." This roadmap sets forth

progresses and challenges in fighting modern slavery in 188 jurisdictions, including 29 in the Asia-Pacific region. And, while there is progress, with more than 20 million estimated trafficking victims in the world and fewer than 45,000 victims identified, we know that we all have a lot more to do. In EAP, we see both sex trafficking and forced labor, even state-sponsored forced labor in the recruitment and the use of child soldiers in some places, and pervasive victimization of migrants seeking better jobs. These are real people, people trapped in slavery, people in the sights of traffickers, people recovering from the trauma of being trafficked. They do not just impact our foreign policy, they touch our conscience.

As you may know, we are working closely with the Vatican as they intensify their engagement on this scourge. And the words of Pope Francis, I think, are very appropriate, when he says that ''Human trafficking is an open wound on the body of contemporary society.''

So, the United States is focused on identifying and seeking justice for victims, supporting survivors, and creating a world where people are no longer subjected to human trafficking. And that means developing common standards and getting governments to step up.

While my written testimony deals in the efforts of a number of jurisdictions in EAP, along with several U.S.-funded initiatives to combat trafficking in the region, I will highlight a few of those efforts and initiatives today.

First, some laudable efforts. The Republic of Korea, Papua-New Guinea, and Solomon Islands all passed legislation to strengthen their legal frameworks. The Federated States of Micronesia initiated a landmark prosecution of a trafficker and implemented a national action plan.

As you mentioned, Senator, we welcomed the formal abolishing of the Reeducation Through Labor System. However, we remain deeply concerned that forced labor persists in some government institutions in China, including Reeducation Through Labor facilities that have been reportedly converted into different types of detention centers. And so, we will be keeping an eye on that. However, there were other issues in China, as well. A second 5-year plan came into operation that included labor trafficking and covered men victims, the accession to the Palermo Protocol, all good signs of forward progress.

Elsewhere, we see mixed efforts. The Government of Burma undertook efforts to improve anti-trafficking response, but some military officials and insurgent militia continue to subject civilians to forced labor and to recruit child soldiers. We are lending our support to help Burma improve its anti-trafficking response through training and a joint action plan on trafficking in persons.

While we saw an uptick in public commitment by the Government of Japan this spring, we are concerned about the steady decline in the number of victims identified in the last 9 years in Japan, despite no evidence of a diminution in the scale of the problem. Thirty-one sex traffickers convicted in 2013, but no labor traffickers. And we know that the traffickers continue to use the Industrial Trainee and Technical Internship Program there to subject victims to forced labor. We will work closely with the Japanese

Government to enhance oversight of this program and improve their anti-trafficking response.

And then there are some countries that did not demonstrate increased efforts to combat trafficking, countries that were downgraded. You mentioned Malaysia and Thailand. In Malaysia, a flawed victim protection regime that detains foreign trafficking victims in government facilities, sometimes for more than a year. We call upon the government to amend its laws and regulations, to improve victim care, to enable all trafficking victims to work and travel outside of these facilities. And we have heard plans announced to allow certain restrictions to be lifted. We hope that we can work with them to turn those promises of future action into credible results.

In Thailand, widespread official complicity continues to be a longstanding problem that remains a significant obstacle to anti-trafficking progress. And whether it is in the fishing industry, forced labor among migrant workers, or the sex industry, the magnitude of the human trafficking problem continues to be of great concern.

I want to close, Senator, with a positive story, though, this year's report on our 10 trafficking-in-persons heroes who are making a difference on the front line. One such hero, Van Ngoc Ta, has personally assisted over 300 trafficking victims of forced labor in Vietnam and sex trafficking victims who had been taken to China. His team works with Vietnamese authorities to liberate victims and then represents them in court against their traffickers. I would offer for the record a recent article about Mr. Van's work. But, his efforts show that homegrown civil society actors can move governments in Southeast Asia and elsewhere, and are an inspiration to us all.

We remain committed to supporting such heroes on the front lines to support and sometimes nudge governments to prevent, protect, and prosecute for our shared goal: a world without slavery.

[The prepared statement of Ambassador CdeBaca follows:]

PREPARED STATEMENT OF AMBASSADOR LUIS CDEBACA

Chairman Cardin, Ranking Member Rubio, members of the subcommittee, thank you very much for giving me the opportunity to share with you the Department of State's latest findings on human trafficking in East Asia and the Pacific Islands. A few weeks ago, Secretary of State John F. Kerry released the 14th annual "Trafficking in Persons Report." This year's 432-page volume discusses the progress and ongoing challenges in fighting trafficking in persons in 188 countries and territories, including 29 countries and territories in the Asia-Pacific region. The world has come a long way in our shared fight against human trafficking over the past 14 years. But, with more than 20 million estimated trafficking victims around the world and fewer than 45,000 victims identified in 2013, we have much more work to do.

Today, I will discuss human trafficking in East Asia and the Pacific, what governments in the region are doing to combat it, and how the Department of State is supporting those efforts. The Department's efforts in Asia require the close collaboration of the Office to Monitor and Combat Trafficking in Persons (the TIP Office) and the Bureau of East Asian and Pacific Affairs. We are grateful for the leadership provided by Assistant Secretary Danny Russel, Principal Deputy Assistant Secretary Scot Marciel, and all of the chiefs of mission throughout the region. Their partnership and collaboration, and the work of their staff on this issue, are making our diplomacy and programs to combat trafficking and assist victims in Asia effective.

REGIONAL OVERVIEW

A staggering portion of the world's trafficking victims come from East Asia. These victims include men, women, and children subjected to both forced labor and sex trafficking. Forced labor occurs in the fishing, agriculture, mining, textile, and domestic service sectors, and in factories that produce other goods. In parts of East Asia, there is also state-sponsored forced labor, including by state militaries. Migrant workers are especially vulnerable to forced labor and debt bondage—in their home countries or upon traveling to other countries for employment. The fishing industry continues to be plagued with forced labor and is in need of additional law enforcement action and anticorruption efforts to curb abuses. Girls and women are forced into prostitution in bars, brothels, massage parlors, and other venues. Sex tourism in some countries fuels the sex trafficking of children. Governments in the region have typically had more success in identifying victims of, and prosecuting cases related to, sex trafficking than labor trafficking; however, more must be done to combat both forms of modern slavery.

Our thematic focus for the 2014 "Trafficking in Persons Report" is the "Journey from Victim to Survivor." The impact of human trafficking is horrifying; those who escape modern slavery struggle to recover, heal, reclaim their lives, and become survivors. It is not an easy path, and true recovery is far from guaranteed. Governments must devote more resources and attention to help victims recover, restore their inner strength and personal voice, and return to their communities as survivors.

Partnerships between governments and the private sector can facilitate this process. As an example, shortly after President Obama's and Secretary Kerry's March 2014 visit to the Vatican, the State Department TIP Office announced its plans to partner with the U.S. Conference of Catholic Bishops and the Apostleship of the Sea to coordinate efforts by the Catholic Church and its partners to combat human trafficking. The project will focus on ramping up capacity around the world to identify and assist victims, particularly those trafficked in maritime labor, which is a significant problem in East Asia and the Pacific.

ACCOMPLISHMENTS AND AREAS FOR IMPROVEMENT

Over the past year, governmental efforts to eliminate human trafficking and assist victims varied dramatically across countries in East Asia and the Pacific.

Some countries and territories undertook laudable anti-trafficking efforts. The Republic of Korea, Papua New Guinea, and the Solomon Islands passed legislation to strengthen their anti-trafficking legal frameworks. The Government of the Federated States of Micronesia initiated a landmark prosecution of an alleged trafficker, declared a national day to spread awareness of trafficking, and implemented a national anti-trafficking action plan. The Chinese National People's Congress ratified a decision to abolish the "Re-education through Labor" (RTL) system, a systemic form of forced labor that had existed in China for decades. Although some media and NGOs report that the government ceased operations at many RTL camps, it has also been reported that the government converted some RTL facilities into different types of detention centers, some of which continue to employ forced labor. We welcome China's decision to abolish the RTL system and its subsequent steps to shutter RTL facilities, but remain deeply concerned that forced labor persists in some government institutions.

Other countries in the region demonstrated mixed efforts to combat trafficking over the past year.

The Government of Burma undertook efforts to improve its anti-trafficking response, but some military officials and insurgent militia continued to subject civilians to forced labor and recruit child soldiers. Burma remains the only country in East Asia on the U.S. Government's Child Soldiers Prevention Act list. We welcome the military's release of 206 children illegally recruited into its ranks over the reporting period, and encourage the Burmese military to continue to take further steps to fulfill commitments it has made under the joint U.N. action plan to end child soldier recruitment.

The United States is partnering with Burma to improve its anti-trafficking efforts, formalized in 2012 through the U.S.-Myanmar Joint Plan on Trafficking in Persons. In support of this joint plan, the TIP Office is funding a $500,000 project to help strengthen Burma's new Anti-Trafficking in Persons Division in the Ministry of Home Affairs by sharing best practices in the area of law enforcement investigation and victim-witness interviewing. Later this year, the TIP Office plans to fund a $700,000 project that will contribute to prevention of trafficking and protection of victims by strengthening institutional and NGO capacities. In this way, the intervention will respond directly to the priority of the Joint Plan of Action to "encourage greater civil society participation in anti-trafficking efforts throughout the country.'' Funding anti-trafficking efforts in Burma will continue to be a priority in FY 2015.

In Cambodia, the government developed guidelines for a standardized, nationwide system for the proactive identification of victims among vulnerable groups. Unfortunately, the government prosecuted and convicted fewer trafficking offenders and identified fewer victims than it did in the previous year. Effectively finalizing and implementing the guidelines will be critical to Cambodia's ability to identify more victims, assist them, and prosecute their traffickers.

We are also concerned that Japan has experienced a steady decline in the number of trafficking victims identified over the past 9 years, despite no evidence of a diminution in the overall scale of the problem. Traffickers continue to use the government's Industrial Trainee and Technical Internship Program (TTIP) to subject victims to forced labor, and the program lacks adequate government oversight. The Japanese Government convicted 31 sex traffickers in 2013—but no labor traffickers. It is working on initiatives to enhance oversight of the TTIP and improve its anti-trafficking response. We look forward to working with the Government of Japan over the coming year as they implement these proposed reforms.

A few countries did not demonstrate increased efforts to combat trafficking over the past year, and they were downgraded in the 2014 TIP Report.

The Government of Malaysia decreased its anti-trafficking law enforcement efforts and made minimal efforts to improve its victim protection regime. In Malaysia, the greatest need is to reform this flawed victim protection regime that detains foreign trafficking victims in government facilities for periods of time that sometimes exceed a year. The Government of Malaysia has announced plans to allow a limited set of foreign trafficking victims to have freedom of movement and the right to work, and for NGOs to operate a government funded shelter. We encourage the government to amend its laws and regulations to improve care for victims and enable all trafficking victims to travel and work outside government facilities. Malaysia identified significantly fewer victims in 2013 than in 2012 and only convicted nine traffickers despite the country's vast trafficking problem. Improving Malaysia's victim protection regime would also be expected to lead to more victims coming forward and providing testimony that leads to more successful prosecutions.

We have been committed to helping Malaysia achieve these goals. The TIP Office is currently programming $750,000 to assist NGOs' anti-trafficking programming in Malaysia, and plans to fund training for Malaysian special prosecutors and judges. We continue to encourage the Government of Malaysia to remove restrictions on NGOs assisting trafficking victims.

Despite improving its anti-trafficking data collection and prosecuting and convicting traffickers, the Government of Thailand failed to address key shortcomings in its anti-trafficking efforts, and its actions continued to be insufficient given the magnitude of the human trafficking problem in Thailand. During the period covered by the 2014 Trafficking in Persons Report, the Thai Government made few efforts to address forced labor and debt bondage among foreign migrant workers—including in the fishing industry, which has a significant proportion of trafficking victims in Thailand. It failed to address widespread official complicity in human trafficking. We continue to call on the Thai Government to take significantly greater steps to protect foreign migrants—including in the fishing and shrimp industries, to punish traffickers who enslave foreign workers, and to prosecute officials complicit in trafficking.

We welcome continued engagement with the Thai Government to address our shared goals: to assist victims, convict traffickers, and prevent future instances of human trafficking from occurring. The TIP Office is currently programming $1.2 million in Thailand to support anti-trafficking activities. This support includes funding to conduct prevention and protection-related activities, especially among tribal populations; enhance Thailand's Department of Special Investigation's ability to investigate trafficking cases; raise awareness and advocate for justice on high-level trafficking cases; coordinate government and NGO activities to combat human trafficking in the nine provinces of the upper northern region of Thailand and their associated Burmese and Lao border regions; and support coordination among the heads of specialist anti-trafficking units in ASEAN. Before the end of the current fiscal year, the TIP Office expects to provide an additional $687,510 to support protection and prosecution-related activities and we anticipate providing continued assistance, pending congressional appropriation in FY 2015 and beyond.

In Laos, the government relied almost entirely on local and international organizations to implement anti-trafficking programs. It continued to prosecute trafficking offenses and convict traffickers, but did not make proactive efforts to identify victims of trafficking. We continue to encourage the government to expeditiously approve Memoranda of Understanding with anti-trafficking organizations to more effectively combat trafficking and coordinate government and NGO efforts. In FY 2010 and FY 2013, our office provided $1 million to the UNODC to assist the Government of Laos with legislative reform of its anti-trafficking law.

The Government of Timor-Leste did not investigate or prosecute any trafficking offenses or convict any traffickers. The government's victim identification efforts remained inadequate, and long-awaited anti-trafficking legislation remained pending.

Finally, one country in the region has continually failed to combat trafficking and has subjected its citizens to trafficking. North Korea did not demonstrate any effort to address human trafficking through prosecution, protection, or prevention measures. The government participated in human trafficking through its use of domestic forced labor camps and its provision of forced labor to foreign governments through bilateral contracts. North Korea also failed to protect victims of trafficking when they were forcibly repatriated from China or other countries.

THE WAY FORWARD

Over the past few weeks, the 2014 "Trafficking in Persons Report" and country tier rankings have received considerable international attention. The report is an important tool to better understand human trafficking in 188 countries and territories around the world and to promote ways to better combat this global problem.

In accordance with the Trafficking Victim's Protection Act, as amended, each country and territory in the report is assigned a tier ranking based on its government's compliance with certain minimum standards to eliminate trafficking. Tier rankings are important. But they are a means to an end, not an end unto themselves. We must not lose sight of the true goal: stopping modern slavery and helping victims of human trafficking. This includes victims like the six young women rescued from a bar by one of our grantees during the devastation of Typhoon Nari in the Philippines, where they had been trafficked and sold as sex slaves. After the rescue and with the storm raging and the power out, our grantee began the interview process by flashlight. The grantee reported that a targeted investment in law enforcement has brought about a nearly 80-percent reduction in the number of girls available for sex in the metropolitan area of Cebu. We agree with our grantee's assessment: "That kind of dramatic reduction can be replicated. It must be replicated." Only with such efforts, and concrete programs to help victims find their voice and reclaim their lives, can we help victims become survivors.

During the rollout of the 2014 report, we honored 10 "Trafficking in Persons Report" Heroes from all over the world who are helping to make a difference. One Hero from Vietnam, Van Ngoc Ta, has personally assisted over 300 trafficking victims of forced labor in Vietnam and sex trafficking in China. Mr. Van's team works with Vietnamese authorities to arrange and implement a plan to facilitate victims' release and represents the victims in court against their traffickers. Mr. Van's tireless efforts have had an impressive positive impact on communities in Vietnam in which he conducts awareness campaigns and meets with leaders and families to educate them on prevention.

These are the types of efforts that must be duplicated around the world. I will now turn to my colleague Principal Deputy Assistant Secretary of State Scot Marciel, with whom I work closely on efforts to combat trafficking. He will discuss U.S. diplomatic engagement on this issue, which is critical to advancing rule of law and human rights as important pillars of our foreign policy.

Senator CARDIN. Well, let me thank both of you, not just for your testimony, but for your commitment in this area. It is well known, and we very much appreciate the fact, that you have been very strong in raising these issues wherever you travel, and making it clear that we expect greater progress. So, I start with that.

But, my first question deals with whether we are making progress or whether we are moving in the wrong direction. And I say that because there were four countries that were downgraded in this report, that are in our region. Only two countries were upgraded. We mentioned China. Let me also mention Micronesia moving from Tier 2 Watch List to Tier 2, which is certainly progress, and we very much acknowledge, in both countries, that progress was made in the right direction.

I have already acknowledged that we have had countries that have been downgraded. Four countries were downgraded in our region: Laos, Malaysia, Thailand, and Timor-Leste.

There were 10 countries that are on Tier 2 that remain on Tier 2, so no progress made. There are four countries that are on Tier 2 Watch List, no progress made: Burma, Cambodia, Marshall Islands, and Solomon Islands. Now, if no progress is made, those countries will be downgraded to Tier 3, as required under the law.

So, my question is, Are we moving in the right direction? Because it looks like the TIP Report would indicate that we have not made progress, when, in fact, there are more countries in worse condition this year than they were in the prior report.

Ambassador CDEBACA. Senator, I actually think that we have seen progress. And some of it is reflected in the report as far as the tiers are concerned. But, even in countries that did not necessarily raise up in a tier, we have seen progress. I hate to use the American grading system as the way that we look at it, but, you know, there is a difference between a ''B'' that is an 80 and a ''B'' that is an 89. They are still both ''B's'' on your report card, but, when you see a student that is starting to make that kind of progress, you can look at that trajectory in a good way.

I think that is what we are seeing with a number of the countries in the region, and especially with the passage, for instance, of the new trafficking legislation in Papua-New Guinea. It did not get quite through the gazetting process, it did not get through the entire process, but is something that we will be looking at in next year's report. And that is a country that is on Tier 3. And yet, we see the government starting to engage. We see that kind of energy, we see an openness, not just to U.S. involvement, but Australian and others who are willing and able to help. So, I think that that is one of the places that we are really looking at.

I think that what we have seen historically is that governments can look at their situation and make a decision to change. We saw that with Vietnam, some years ago. And, at this point, I think that we very much see them as a solid Tier 2 country. There was a few years when we would look at it and, frankly, we would be wondering, Is this still really a Tier 2 country? Should they be back to Tier 2 Watch List? Kind of, where are they? We are seeing that solidifying as they are starting to work with civil society organizations like Blue Dragon, as they are starting to look at labor trafficking instead of just sex trafficking.

So, I think that we are seeing what, to us, looks like progress. I think that the four downgrades actually—in some ways, not only does that reflect the lack of progress in some of those countries, but it reflects good, solid reporting on the part of our Embassies and otherwise. As we get more information, as we are engaging with them, we are learning more and more about the trafficking situation in these countries. So, the notion of downgrades is not something that we necessarily see as a failure in the region. We see it as honest reporting that allows us and you and others to make a difference. And we have already heard that, in the press coverage, in some of the public statements that we are seeing out of Malaysia and other places, a commitment to going out and working.

Senator CARDIN. Well, I would just observe, we absolutely believe that the TIP evaluations are honest reporting and honest grading. This is accurate grading that we expect that will continue.

But, having said that, it is disturbing to see, with all of the global attention on trafficking—and there has been a tremendous focus on trafficking issues globally, not just the United States of America—and with all the technical support that is now available to deal with improving the trafficking issues, it is disturbing to see, in the jurisdiction of this subcommittee, East Asia and the Pacific, that, with all the priorities being given, we have not made the type of advancements that I think is expected.

Now, there are three countries here that are TPP aspirants. Two have dealt with their trafficking issues. Vietnam has been under tremendous focus in this committee, and they have consistently been a Tier 2 country. Now, we would like to see them at Tier 1, but they have made progress on the trafficking issues. I was in Vietnam this year, and we talked about the trafficking issues, and the country is very much focused on dealing with the issues.

Brunei, which has serious human rights issues in trafficking, they have been consistent.

Malaysia moved in the wrong direction. What does that mean, as far as they are ready for TPP? Are they ready for TPP, if they cannot deal with their trafficking issues? It raises a question to me.

So, Secretary Marciel, are we making progress? Are we moving in the wrong direction?

Ambassador MARCIEL. Thank you, Mr. Chairman.

Clearly, we have a lot more work to do in Malaysia; and, more importantly, the Malaysians have a lot of work to do on trafficking, particularly their treatment of trafficking victims. It is a big priority in the relationship, for sure.

In terms of TPP, one of—I mean, the whole idea of TPP, as you know, in addition to opening markets, is setting high standards, including in labor. And, I mean, obviously, the negotiations are still underway, but the intent is to have a very strong labor chapter in there. So, we actually think the TPP process should reinforce—even though it does not have a TIP chapter, per se, it does have very high standards, including on labor. So, I think it should reinforce the effort. But, clearly, the Malaysians have a lot more to do.

Senator CARDIN. One more observation on that. Many of us support a very high standard—ILO standards in regards to labor in TPP, but we also want to see that within the core agreement, with enforceability within the core agreement, which we did not have in CAFTA. So, the TIP Report and the spotlight of the TIP Report was not enough to get Malaysia at the level that it needed to be. It is just a clear signal, at least to this Senator, that the TPP needs to have enforceable labor commitments, because we have not been able to make the progress by just putting a spotlight through the TIP Report.

Let me ask one more question. Senator Rubio had explained to me that he was going to be late getting here, for personal reasons, and I fully understand that. I want to give him a moment to catch his breath and thank him so much, because he has been one of the real leaders, in the United States Senate, on trafficking issues and on human rights issues in East Asia and the Pacific, and I very much appreciate his commitment to our mutual agenda to underscore and highlight these matters.

I was in Moldova last week, and their leadership is really committed to human rights issues, and I think they have made a lot of progress. I know it is not one of our countries. But, it was interesting. They identified, as the core area for improvement on trafficking, would be to deal with corruption. And they have dealt with corruption. They have put some of their judges in jail because they were not enforcing the laws dealing with trafficking. Those who trafficked knew they could get away with their activities. But, Moldova has made a commitment to change that.

In the countries of East Asia and Pacific, particularly those that need to improve on trafficking, they have significant challenges on dealing with corruption. How well is that understood in these countries, that in order to deal with modern-day slavery, they have to deal with the corruption in their system?

Ambassador MARCIEL. Well, Mr. Chairman, I will start.

I think, for a lot of these countries—and I have spent quite a bit of time in many of them—corruption is a huge issue. In some cases, it is arguably the biggest issue in the eyes of the people, not only because of the impact on trafficking, but the impact on people's daily lives, writ large, and certainly on rule of law and people's desire for justice. So, I think the problem of corruption is very widely understood, and there is—in the places I have been, there is, you know, tremendous public pressure and societal pressure on governments and political leaders to improve, to clean up on corruption, including because of its relationship to trafficking in persons.

In my experience, it is a difficult challenge to tackle. It requires a tremendous amount of political will and a lot of effort over time. But, it is critical, not only on the trafficking front, but if these countries are going to achieve economic development and the justice that their people demand.

Senator CARDIN. Thank you.

Senator Rubio.

Senator RUBIO. thank you, Mr. Chairman, for holding this hearing, and both of you for being here.

I want to just open—and I apologize for being a few minutes late, but let me just begin with a statement about all this.

Human trafficking, of course, is a monstrous crime which plagues the entire world, including, quite frankly, my home State of Florida, which is one of the top three destinations for human trafficking in the United States. Unfortunately, the populations of East Asia and the Pacific region are disproportionally affected by trafficking. The International Labor Organization estimates that there are currently 7.9 million victims of forced labor in the Asia-Pacific region. The recently released 2014 Trafficking in Persons Report includes four Asian countries in the worst-of-the-worst Tier 3 category: Malaysia, North Korea, Papua-New Guinea, and Thailand. Numerous other Asian nations find themselves near Tier 3, in the Tier 2 Watch List. That includes Burma, Cambodia, China, Laos—the list goes on and on.

Today, we will explore, and have been exploring, the causes of human trafficking in the region, as well as the governments in that region and the responses that they have had in compliance with the laws and the expectations upon them. And the United States has always been, and will continue to be, a leader in combating modern-day slavery in the world. And I appreciate the work both of you do with regards to that. We must highlight this issue, hopefully at every level, when working on a bilateral and multilateral levels, with countries in this important region.

And then, I want to thank you, Mr. Chairman, for holding this hearing on this important topic. And I want to thank the witnesses for being here.

I was going to start with Secretary Marciel. I wanted to ask you, How does our anti—and you may have answered this already, so I apologize, but—How does the anti-trafficking platform—how does that work with the other priorities that we have in the region, such as defense or economic issues? How do we coordinate those sometimes competing interests, I suppose?

Ambassador MARCIEL. Thank you, Senator Rubio.

Yes, it is a very good question and a challenge for us. I mean, I guess what I would say is, in all of our relationships in the region, we obviously focus a lot on the diplomatic relationship, building people-to-people ties, trade relations, all of these sorts of things. But, in every country where we see problems on human rights and/or trafficking, more specifically, this is another important piece of what we do, and we make clear, in our discussions with government officials, that, you know, we want to build a closer relationship, but our ability to do so depends certainly, to a significant extent, on their willingness and ability to address these concerns, whether it is broad human rights or trafficking in persons. And then, in addition to that, in many of these countries, we will have programs—either, you know, training prosecutors or police or judges, or often working with civil society, because civil society's role is critical in this, both exposing the problem, but putting pressure on governments to do more, but then, actually helping victims. So, it is a combination of diplomatic pressure and making it a priority plus specific programs. And I know Ambassador CdeBaca can talk more about that.

Ambassador CDEBACA. Senator, I think that one of the things that we are really looking at is how it works with our priorities both around rule of law and human rights, and bringing those two together. I think that often human trafficking has been seen in the—especially in Southeast Asia—as a transnational problem of moving people. And one of the things that I think that we have seen often because—just to get into the weeds—it is the same reporting officers in our embassies that are doing the human rights report, as well as the trafficking report. It brings a little bit of a harder edge to the human rights approach, and it brings a little human rights to the law enforcement approach. And I think that that has enabled us to have a conversation that is moving into each of these countries. We are starting to be able to deal with the Thai person who is enslaved in Thailand, the Vietnamese person enslaved in Vietnam. Whereas, 5 years ago, I think a lot of the countries were only focused upon the cross-border.

What that is doing is, it is allowing us to introduce other aspects of rule of law, whether it is the corruption issue, whether it is general judicial training, access to justice, et cetera. And I think that that kind of lifts all boats, that rising tide.

So, we are trying to make sure that it is incorporated in that way.

Senator RUBIO. Let me ask you this. I have gotten—a number of NGOs have expressed concern that, during the Trafficking in Persons Report, the regional bureaus include political considerations in the tier rankings and press the TIP office to not downgrade certain countries. Is that accurate? Is that happening?

Whoever has the answer.

Ambassador MARCIEL. Senator, actually, Ambassador CdeBaca and I sat down, on a number of occasions after our teams had worked through these, to go through the countries. There were, you know, some countries that we all agreed clearly fell into one category, and there were others that were a little bit closer. You know, was it a strong "B" or a weak "A minus," as Ambassador CdeBaca said? And, basically, we went through and discussed—I would not say "debated," but just discussed what the countries have done and what they had not done. And our conversations were all about what had been done on trafficking. So, we were not saying, "No, but—you know, that, yes, they did not do anything on trafficking, but they are good friends, you cannot downgrade them." We did not have that conversation. It was purely——

Senator RUBIO. So, the political considerations are not used in the TIP process to distort the tier rankings.

Ambassador CDEBACA. I think actually they—we do—we, collectively, the State Department, do a pretty good job of keeping this focused on trafficking. And it helps that there is real criteria, so you cannot really fudge it, in that sense.

Senator RUBIO. Because I am—you know, what I am getting—I mean, some people are concerned—and I am glad to hear your statement here today; it is important to have that on the record—that, in fact, there are some countries, where, because of certain geopolitical issues, there might be some internal pressure not to downgrade them or to move them off their current tier ranking. But, your statement here today is that because of the criteria that is in place, that is not happening.

Ambassador CDEBACA. That is correct, Senator. And I think if you look at the fact that long-time friend and treaty ally Thailand was downgraded, as well as Malaysia, where the President had just visited, have a very good relationship—they were both downgraded.

Senator RUBIO. Okay.

And, Ambassador, let me ask this question about China. And again, I apologize, you may have answered this already before. In the 2013 report, China was automatically downgraded to the lowest level of Tier 3 because it had been on the Tier 2 Watch List for 2 consecutive years—and, by the way, waived for 2 more years—and had not made any improvements. In the 2014 report, they were upgraded back to the Tier 2 Watch List. So, what exactly did China do—what improvements did they make in that reporting period that allowed them to be upgraded to Tier 2?

Ambassador CDEBACA. Senator, there are a few things that we were really looking at last year, especially the Reeducation Through Labor Camps, the state-sponsored forced labor that we saw in China. And that was one of our biggest recommendations for the Chinese. And we saw movement from them this last year.

Senator RUBIO. I am sorry to interject. Is that actually happening, or are they running that program under a different name? I mean, is there real evidence that they have dismantled those programs?

Ambassador CDEBACA. We have seen evidence that they have dismantled the main program, but we are concerned that it not be shunted over to other reeducation camps, whether it is drugs or other morality offenses, or things like that. And it is something that we are very much looking at very closely, because I think we share the skepticism, no—to make sure that this is a trust-but-verify.

Senator RUBIO. Okay.

Ambassador CDEBACA. On the other hand, we see other things that they have done, such as acceding to the Palermo Protocol, the issuance of a new 5-year plan, that directly went to some of the issues that we had raised. Their previous structure did not allow for the identification of male victims at all, so they were having cases where men would be brought out of—mentally retarded or drug-addicted men brought out of a brickkiln, where they had been held for 5 years, kidnapped off the street, and they were not charging that as trafficking, because their definitions, their laws, just did not see those men as trafficking victims, because they were not women being taken across an international border. They have changed that now. They have changed the structure so that you are bringing in the All China Women's Federation to do victim protection at the beginning of the cases.

All of those, we think, are enough of a change that we did not feel that a Tier 3 was appropriate for China. We are not saying, however, that this is a feel-good story. This is not a Tier 2, this is certainly not a Tier 1. This is just enough to come off of Tier 3, and we are going to be really looking at this.

Senator RUBIO. Let me just highlight one more thing that I am hearing from NGOs with regards to China. And that is that many students from Chinese vocational schools are being forced to work in factories as interns, performing work that is not related to their major and, quite frankly, has no educational benefit. These students risk not receiving their diploma if they refuse to work. Is that something that we are looking at and taking into account, that they are using these sorts of forced labor situations hidden and disguised as some sort of vocational training program?

Ambassador CDEBACA. We have not seen it necessarily rise to the level of abuse that we have expressed concern about in the Japanese Training and Technical Internship Program or in the Uzbek use of the students for the cotton harvest, and others. But, it is something that we are looking at and something that we continue to keep an eye on.

Again, we do not want there to be ways to try to get around getting rid of the RTL camps by coming up with other forced labor situations.

Senator RUBIO. And is that okay?

In your testimony, you noted that foreign governments tend to focus—and I think this was you—yes, Ambassador, it was you that said this in your testimony, that foreign governments—and you alluded to a it, a second ago—they tend to focus their anti-trafficking efforts on sex trafficking, which is horrifying, but there is also the issue of labor trafficking that has not—sometimes people do not think about that as equally horrifying, in many cases. So, how are we engaging with foreign governments—and you started to touch upon that a moment ago—can you describe how we engage with foreign governments to explain that they are—that—because that is where I think you are running into a lot of the situations you just outlined, a moment ago. What are we doing to kind of create more awareness on their part that labor trafficking is also trafficking—that sex trafficking is horrifying, and we want to put a stop to it, but also the labor trafficking element of it, as well?

Ambassador CDEBACA. I think this is actually the culture change that we are moving into with these governments. A lot of folks in Southeast Asia have had a real learning curve, especially around the domestic servant issues, whether it is in Singapore, Hong Kong, other places, Malaysia, where there is such a strong culture of bringing in foreign domestic servants. Those cases often, when they manifest, to the degree that they are ever dealt with, get dealt with as assault cases. And so, we have been going in, almost on a case-by-case basis, and doing the legal arguments with these governments to say, "No, this case, under international law, is a trafficking case."

What we have also been doing, frankly, is to then harness the anti-trafficking community in the United States so that we end up getting experts, whether it is folks from the Freedom Network or other consortia of the people who are doing the hard work, and we send them out to the countries. Some of the folks from the Florida coalition, for instance, have been able to travel in that way. And I think that what it is doing is, it is starting to get to the prosecutors and the police. I think the next step is going to be the judges. The judges do not, still, seem to understand this. But, we are kind of lining them up and knocking them down, one by one.

The Thailand downgrade, I think, will speak volumes in the region, because we made it very clear in the narrative that there had been work done, over the last year, against human trafficking. It just had been almost exclusively done in the sex industry. And, while we want that, and while we laud the people who are doing that in Thailand, the crushing numbers actually show up in forced labor. And the fact that we are willing to downgrade such an important country largely over labor trafficking, hopefully sends that signal.

Senator RUBIO. I just have a brief comment and a quick question.

Senator CARDIN. Sure.

Senator RUBIO. No, just one more point. You just spoke about the Thailand thing a moment ago. Just here domestically, I think one of the most important things we need to continue to do—and this is more of an editorial statement—is, we need to make it very clear there is nothing culturally acceptable about going to these other countries, as Americans, and participating in these sorts of things. I mean, there is this attitude that I have run into now and then, where things we would never do in this country is okay if we do it somewhere else, because in those countries it is culturally accept-

able in some way. And I think you have seen this reflected sometimes in popular culture, but even anecdotally among people.

And I think one of the things we have to make very clear, that
there is nothing acceptable about Americans going abroad to one
of these countries and going into brothels at all, not to mention
those that have people underage working there. And I think that
is important to point out, because we do find the presence of West-
erners and Americans frequenting some of these places that we
have talked about in the sex trafficking industry, and we should
truly try to stigmatize that in our society.

The last question I had—this is for you, Mr. Secretary—as the
United States considers increased military engagement with
Burma, how is the issue of child soldiers factoring into those conversations? And will that be a priority for us, moving forward, as
we have those conversations on increasing that military relationship?

Ambassador MARCIEL. Senator, yes, very much so. There is a lot
that we want the Burmese military to do as part of the country's
broader reform effort, and we have highlighted to them the issue
of child soldiers, as well as use of forced labor. We have seen some
movement—I think there were a couple hundred child soldiers who
were released—and a willingness to talk about it. A lot more that
needs to be done. Our Assistant Secretary for Human Rights, Tom
Malinowski, along with our Deputy PACOM Commander, General
Crutchfield, were in Burma a couple of weeks ago, met with the
military and talked about a range of human rights issues, including this. So, we have made it very clear, this is hugely important,
and we will continue to do that.

Senator CARDIN. Senator Rubio, thank you for your questions
and your support here, and your leadership.

You are absolutely right about being complicitous in trafficking.
And you are right about Americans traveling abroad visiting brothels. We have taken strong leadership with our military to make it
clear that they cannot at all participate in those types of activities,
and that what it is doing is undermining the security of the United
States and the principles that we believe in. That has been part of
our policy, and I thank you for underscoring that today.

The challenge on forced labor is, How do you deal with consumers who want to know if the products that they are consuming
have been produced, in part, by forced labor? And that is an issue
that we can all do a better job in figuring out how we can connect
consumers to what is happening so that they are not participating
in trafficking activities through their purchases, or supporting it.

I just want to underscore one point that you raised. And that is
the objectivity of the TIP Report. The two people who are at the
witness table have been critical in making it clear that politics does
not play a role in this evaluation, that this is an objective test used
to help countries get the help they need to improve their record on
trafficking. And this report is very objective.

Let me just read, from one Pacific country, the beginning. It
says, "Is a source, transit, and destination country for men, women,
and children, both citizens and foreign nationals subjected to sex
trafficking and forced labor, including domestic servitude. Trafficking can occur in both legal and illegal industries or markets,

including in brothels, escort services, massage parlors, strip clubs, street prostitution, hotel services, hospitality, sales crews, agriculture, manufacturing, and janitorial services, construction, health, and elder care and domestic service.''

That is the beginning report on a Tier 1 country, the United States. So, it is pretty clear that every country can improve in its record.

Well, let me just read from Malaysia, which is now a Tier 3 country and a TPP aspirant, ''Where Malaysia is a destination and, to a lesser extent, a source and transit country for men, women, and children subjected to forced labor, and women and children subjected to sex trafficking, the overwhelming majority of trafficking victims are among the estimated 2 million documented and 2 million or more undocumented foreign workers in Malaysia. Foreign workers typically migrate willingly to Malaysia from other countries in Asia, primarily Indonesia, Bangladesh, the Philippines, Nepal, Burma, Cambodia, Vietnam, and India, Thailand, and Laos, in search of greater economic opportunity. Some of the migrants subsequently encounter forced labor or debt bondage at the hands of their employer, employment agents, or informal labor recruitments.''

I mention that because Malaysia is an aspirant country for TPP. And I must tell you, Secretary Marciel, yes, I believe we can elevate that through a strong labor provision within the TPP, but it has got to be enforceable. And I have underscored that point. We have yet to enter into a trade agreement that had enforceable labor provisions. We had labor provisions; they have not been enforceable.

So, I can tell you, this Senator is going to be watching very closely, and the fact that we have not seen the type of progress in Malaysia is of great concern to me.

I want to ask one final question, if I might. And that is, in Europe and Central Asia, the United States and Canada, through OSCE, participate in a robust effort to elevate trafficking and technical support to improve actions against trafficking within the OSCE framework. And there is a formal part of OSCE that deals with anti-trafficking measures.

I do not see a similar commitment within the ASEAN nations. Now, we are not a participating state. We do have observer status, and we do participate, but not as a full member of ASEAN. Could ASEAN be stronger in its commitments on dealing with the trafficking issues? And what can the United States do about that?

Ambassador CDEBACA. I think that it could be, and we are seeing a lot of energy for that among the different member states. What the United States can and has done is, for the first time now, we are actually bringing together the ASEAN Secretariat on Human Trafficking, through the Transnational Organized Crime efforts, with U.S. funding, to actually have the beginning of a Secretariat for anti-trafficking work. It kind of mirrors the early years of the Stability Pact Task Force that then grew into the anti-trafficking unit at OSCE headquarters. We are very pleased to see that the immediate past Special Representative for Trafficking, Maria Grazia Giamarinaro, is now going to be the United Nations Special Rapporteur for Trafficking. So, that OSCE experience is going to be available to the entire world through our support. But, we are also then trying to replicate that model at the beginning stage, in working with the folks at ASEAN. And, to that end, we are in the planning stages of bringing folks together during the Burmese Presidency to have a discussion across ASEAN and with the United States and other supporters this fall so that we can start working on it. I cannot guarantee you that it will end up as formal or successful as what we saw in the OSCE, but I think it is certainly a seed that we can germinate.

Senator CARDIN. Thank you.

Mr. Secretary.

Ambassador MARCIEL. Mr. Chairman, if I could just add, in addition to what Ambassador CdeBaca said, the ASEAN—first, I agree, ASEAN can and should do more. I think they are beginning to move—a little bit slowly, but moving. They are working on drafting an ASEAN convention on trafficking in persons and a regional plan of action. And we are engaging with them. When Assistant Secretary Danny Russell met with his ASEAN counterparts in Burma, I think it was a month ago, he raised this issue, stressed the importance of it. And we are funding, through Ambassador CdeBaca's office and the American Bar Association, a rule-of-law initiative, a program to work with ASEAN to help improve their anti-trafficking units.

So, there is potential there, and they are beginning to move down the path. But, they have a ways to go to catch up to OSCE.

Senator CARDIN. I thank you.

Senator Rubio?

Let me thank both of you, again, for your commitment on this issue and for your frankness with this committee. And we very much look forward to working in partnership with you to make progress to end trafficking, our modern-day slavery.

Thank you.

We will now move to our second panel. We have Ms. Neha Misra, senior specialist for migration and human trafficking at the Solidarity Center, AFL–CIO, an international workers' rights NGO based in Washington, DC. Previously, Ms. Misra was the deputy county director and program manager for the Solidarity Center, Counter-Trafficking in Persons Project in Indonesia and served as the director of the Solidarity Center Democracy Project in Indonesia.

We have, also, Mr. Jesse Eaves, senior policy advisor for child protection at World Vision. He has worked at the World Vision, focuses on issues of child protection, including child soldiers, exploitation, child labor, child trafficking, and child sexual exploitation.

It is good to have both of you with us today. You have heard our comments during the first panel, so I think you know our concerns.

As I have indicated before, your full statements will be made part of the record. You may proceed as you wish.

And we will start with Ms. Misra.

STATEMENT OF NEHA MISRA, SENIOR SPECIALIST, MIGRATION AND HUMAN TRAFFICKING, SOLIDARITY CENTER, WASHINGTON, DC

Ms. MISRA. Thank you very much, Senator Cardin.

I just, first, wanted to start by not just saying thank you for inviting us to testify today, but also thank you specifically to the Senate Foreign Relations Committee and then directly, Senator Rubio and yourself, Senator Cardin, for the leadership that you have shown on addressing issues of human trafficking. And, as you mentioned, not just issues of trafficking for sexual exploitation, but also labor trafficking. The committee and both of your leadership on this issue is very much appreciated.

Working to promote and protect worker rights globally with programs in more than 60 countries and through 26 field offices, the Solidarity Center's anti-trafficking programs scan the globe. And, while each country we work in has its own set of unique circumstances and problems, we have found a common link between systematic worker rights violations and human trafficking. This is particularly acute in the three countries on which I will focus my testimony today: Thailand, Malaysia, and Cambodia.

We commend the State Department for downgrading Thailand and Malaysia to Tier 3 in this year's TIP Report, and ranking Cambodia on the Tier 2 Watch List. These rankings reflect the reality that Solidarity Center and our partners on the ground in these countries deal with every day—specifically, the lack of progress by these governments in the identification and protection of victims, particularly migrant workers; prosecution of perpetrators, especially labor recruiters and employers; and prevention and deterrence of labor trafficking. We believe the tier rankings should be just the first step. The U.S. Government and U.S. companies conducting business in these countries have additional tools at their disposal to push Thailand, Malaysia, and Cambodia to implement concrete and effective initiatives to combat human trafficking for forced labor, debt bondage, and other forms of labor exploitation.

There are three main factors involved in labor trafficking in Thailand, Malaysia, and in Cambodia that I would like to highlight.

First, a common element of the trafficking problem in these three countries is the particular vulnerability of migrant workers to forced labor and the lack of political will in the governments to do much about it. The potential profits to be made from the labor migration business in the region by government officials, employers, employment agencies, and labor recruiters seem to trump initiatives to combat migrant workers' vulnerability. In all three countries, unsafe migration processes and the lack of labor law and other legal protections for migrant workers make them an easy target for traffickers.

In 2008, my organization, the Solidarity Center, released a report entitled "The True Cost of Shrimp: How the Shrimp Industry Workers in Bangladesh and Thailand Pay the Price for Affordable Shrimp." Thailand is one of the main exporters of shrimp to the United States. The report highlighted how companies in Thailand systematically use the lack of labor rights and weak labor law enforcement to exploit, traffic, and put Burmese migrant workers into forced labor and debt bondage. Six years later, little progress has been made. Despite the overwhelming evidence of a high vulnerability of migrant workers in Thailand to trafficking, the Thai

Government has actually implemented measures that increase migrant worker vulnerability to labor trafficking.

The recent military coup in Thailand also raises concerns. While it is too early to tell how the current military government will respond to the human trafficking crisis, there have been reports of a crackdown on undocumented migrant workers, with thousands of Cambodian workers fleeing over the border from Thailand to Cambodia.

Migrant workers in Malaysia face a similar situation. With migrant workers comprising nearly 30 percent of the workforce, Malaysia is one of the largest destination countries for migrant workers in Asia. At the same time, migrant workers in Malaysia routinely have their rights violated, with little recourse under Malaysian law and policies. Similar to the Thai Government, the Malaysian Government has actually implemented policies to increase migrant workers' vulnerability to trafficking.

Cambodia is primarily an origin country for migrant workers, as the Cambodian Government promotes labor migration as a way to increase revenue and address high unemployment. Yet, the government fails to monitor the recruitment process or protect its workers overseas. Cambodian officials have been tied to actual trafficking of victims over the Thai border.

The second factor among the three countries is the lack of investigations, prosecutions, and convictions for forced labor, which is linked to corruption, complacency, and complicity of government officials. There have been ridiculously few prosecutions for forced labor in these countries. And even when prosecutions are brought, they usually result in small fines and jail time, and perpetrators are often let out on bail.

The third factor that I would like to talk about is the lack of economic pressure by governments and businesses to eliminate forced labor and other forms of labor trafficking in supply chains. Clearly, Malaysia, Thailand, and Cambodia are important bilateral partners for the United States. Thailand is one of the largest exporters of seafood to the United States, and ready-made garments come into the United States from Malaysia and Cambodia. Given the significant problem of trafficking of migrant workers along these supply chains, it is likely that products made with forced labor are ending up on retail shelves in the United States.

Given I am running out of time, I just very quickly wanted to mention a few recommendations that I hope you will ask me about in the question-and-answer period.

Senator Cardin, you have already mentioned my first and primary one, and that is using trade agreements as a way to prevent trafficking in the region. The TPP is a prime example of this, and, as you mentioned, we believe strongly that labor standards in the TPP and other trade agreements should include the same enforcement and dispute resolution mechanisms as other provisions, like international property rights.

We also feel strongly that Congress should encourage the U.S. Trade Representative to suspend GSP and other trade preferences for any country that does not effectively address forced labor. The AFL–CIO recently filed a GSP petition against Thailand, asking the USTR to suspend Thailand's GSP status based on issues of forced labor and exploitation of migrant workers in the country.

I also—just two more quick ones—one is, we need to regulate labor recruiters around the world. The U.S. Congress can take a lead in this by passing legislation to regulate foreign labor recruiters who bring migrant workers into the United States.

Again, I would like to thank both Senator Cardin and Senator Rubio on helping to pass, last year, Subtitle F as part of S. 744, which regulates labor recruiters and has great provisions on the elimination of fees. We hope that this bill can get passed in the House and become law and serve as a model for countries such as Thailand and Malaysia.

I will just end by saying a few other things that we need to do is look at the Tariff Act of 1930 and the consumptive demand exception. When you talked about consumers, Senator Cardin, and the role that they can play, there are absolutely products being made with forced labor that are in our grocery stores, in our retail stores. And Thai shrimp may be one of these. A way that we can help consumers figure out what to do is to enforce the Tariff Act and stop these products from being exported into the United States. But, without getting rid of the consumptive demand exception, we will be unable to do that.

We also need to put more pressure on companies to map their supply chains and multinational corporations as buyers who have the economic pressure that they can put on the suppliers in countries such as Thailand, Malaysia, and Cambodia, to exert that pressure. And we feel one way to do that is through the Business Supply Chain Transparency on Trafficking and Slavery Act of 2014.

Thank you very much.

[The prepared statement of Ms. Misra follows:]

PREPARED STATEMENT OF NEHA MISRA

Mr. Chairman, Senator Rubio, and other distinguished members of the Senate Foreign Relations Subcommittee on East Asian and Pacific Affairs, thank you for the opportunity to present the Solidarity Center's perspective on the scope of human trafficking in East Asia and the Pacific. We appreciate the committee's attention to this horrific human rights abuse and particularly its emphasis on the labor issues related to trafficking in the region. I ask that my full written statement be put into the record, and I will summarize my main points now.

My name is Neha Misra. I am the Senior Specialist for Migration and Human Trafficking at the Solidarity Center. We are an international nongovernmental organization (NGO) that promotes and protects worker rights globally, working in more than 60 countries through 26 field offices. The Solidarity Center is an allied organization of the AFL–CIO, and a member of the Alliance to End Slavery and Trafficking (ATEST). Building upon more than 20 years of experience in the areas of child labor, migrant worker exploitation, and supply chain accountability, the Solidarity Center raises awareness about the prevalence and underlying causes of forced labor and other forms of trafficking for labor exploitation, and implements programs with partners from myriad sectors to combat the problem. These programs include initiatives that address each of the four "Ps" that have become part of the anti-trafficking paradigm: prevention, protection of victims, prosecution (or as we prefer to describe it, "rule of law"), and partnerships. The Solidarity Center has the unique ability to work across borders, in both countries of origin and destination for trafficked workers, as we have long-term on the ground relationships with local partners. We have implemented antihuman trafficking programs in countries such as China (Hong Kong), India, Indonesia, Malaysia, Nepal, Pakistan, the Philippines, Sri Lanka, Thailand, Jordan, Kuwait, Qatar, Kenya, Sierra Leone, Moldova, and the Dominican Republic.

The Solidarity Center's anti-trafficking programs span the globe. And while each country we work in has its own set of unique circumstances and problems, we have found common themes. Human trafficking and forced labor have, at their core, violations of worker rights and lack of labor standards and protections for workers. Whether its low-wage workers in sectors such as domestic work or construction, migrant workers[1] toiling on palm oil plantations, or other marginalized groups such as poor women workers or child laborers, human trafficking is a worker rights issue because it is linked to various forms of labor exploitation. It is one of the worst forms of worker abuse. This link between worker rights violations and human trafficking is particularly acute in the three countries on which I will focus my testimony today: Thailand, Malaysia, and Cambodia.

Although U.S. and international definitions of human trafficking clearly include forced labor, many policymakers and much of the general public around the world associate trafficking only with forced prostitution or commercial sexual exploitation. We continue to struggle to get governments to respond adequately to the problem of labor trafficking. Victims of trafficking for labor exploitation frequently go unidentified. Immigration officials regularly categorize migrant workers who are trafficking victims as undocumented workers and deport them. Police and labor inspectors often view involuntary servitude or debt bondage in sectors such as agriculture, construction, manual labor, and manufacturing as worker rights abuses that do not require their intervention. And governments have prosecuted shockingly few cases of forced labor globally. Thailand, Malaysia, and Cambodia are prime examples of this.

We commend the U.S. Department of State for downgrading Thailand and Malaysia to Tier 3 in its annual Trafficking in Persons Report, and ranking Cambodia on the Tier 2 Watch List. After 4 years on the Tier 2 Watch List, U.S. law required that Thailand and Malaysia be either upgraded or downgraded. The Solidarity Center and ATEST are ardent supporters of the U.S. Department of State's Office to Monitor and Combat Trafficking in Persons (J/TIP) because we have witnessed the crucial global leadership role that J/TIP plays in promoting the eradication of trafficking and forced labor. We are also strong supporters of the annual TIP Report, which in recent years has documented an exponential increase in trafficking for forced labor, debt bondage and other severe forms of labor exploitation.

Over the years, however, there have been specific country cases where political considerations rather than trafficking eradication were brought into play in the tier rankings. This undermines the credibility of the TIP Report. The State Department 2012 Inspector General's Inspection of the Office to Monitor and Combat Trafficking in Persons found: ''. . . there is an inherent difference in perspective between J/TIP and the regional bureaus, which stems from J/TIP's mandated responsibility to implement the TVPA [Trafficking Victims Protection Act] and the regional bureaus' responsibilities for overall bilateral relations.''[2] We are pleased to see, however, that the narratives and tier rankings for Thailand, Malaysia, and Cambodia in the 2014 TIP Report reflect the reality that the Solidarity Center and our partners on the ground deal with every day—specifically, the lack of progress by the governments of these countries in the identification and protection of victims, prosecution of perpetrators (especially labor recruiters and employers), and prevention and deterrence of labor trafficking.[3]

As I will discuss below, we believe the tier rankings should be just the first step. The United States Government and U.S. companies conducting business in these countries have additional tools at their disposal to push Thailand, Malaysia and Cambodia to implement concrete and effective initiatives to combat human trafficking for forced labor, debt bondage, and other forms of labor exploitation. It is past time to use these tools, as millions of workers continue to face vulnerability to human trafficking in the region.

Trafficking for labor exploitation is pervasive in all three countries. There are three main factors involved in labor trafficking in Thailand, Malaysia, and Cambodia I would like to highlight:

1. The high vulnerability of migrant workers to human trafficking, and the lack of political will among the governments to take serious measures to combat it.

2. Lack of investigations, prosecutions, and convictions for forced labor (linked to corruption, complacency and even complicity of government officials in labor trafficking).

3. The lack of economic pressure by governments and businesses to eliminate forced labor (and other forms of labor trafficking) in the supply chains of products exported to the United States and other global destinations.

THE HIGH VULNERABILITY OF MIGRANT WORKERS TO HUMAN TRAFFICKING

A common element of the trafficking problem in Thailand, Malaysia, and Cambodia is the particular vulnerability of migrant workers to forced labor, debt bondage, and involuntary servitude, and the lack of political will in the governments to do much about it. The potential profits to be made from the global labor migration business—by government officials, employers, employments agencies and labor recruiters—seem to trump initiatives to combat migrant workers vulnerability.

Unsafe migration processes and the lack of labor law and other legal protections for migrant workers make them an easy target for traffickers. Migrant workers are often explicitly excluded from the protection of labor and other laws—either because of their immigration status or because of the sector they work in (such as domestic work). Traffickers—in the form of labor recruiters and employers—take advantage of this exclusion and of the failure to enforce and monitor laws when they do exist, increasing the vulnerability of migrant workers to human trafficking.

Moreover, employers, businesses, and multinational corporations increasingly rely on foreign labor recruiters or brokers to facilitate the movement of workers from one country to another (and even manage workers in the workplace after arrival). Recruiters are often complicit with or directly involved in trafficking of workers. They regularly charge exorbitant fees for their services, forcing workers into debt bondage, falsifying documents, and deceiving workers about their terms and conditions of work, increasing their vulnerability to human trafficking. Labor recruiters play a major role in the trafficking of migrant workers throughout Asia.

Thailand

The majority of human trafficking victims in Thailand are migrant workers. There are an estimated 3 to 4 million migrant workers in Thailand comprising about 10 percent of the country's workforce. Most come from neighboring countries, with the majority from Burma. Many, if not most, of these migrant workers are undocumented. Migrant workers in Thailand (men, women, and children) toil in almost all sectors of the economy, but especially commercial fishing, fishing-related industries like seafood processing, low-end garment production, factories/manufacturing, and domestic work. They perform dangerous, difficult, and dirty jobs—and there is high demand for their cheap labor among Thai employers.

In 2008, the Solidarity Center released a report as part of its Degradation of Work series entitled, ''The True Cost of Shrimp: How Shrimp Industry Workers in Bangladesh and Thailand Pay the Price for Affordable Shrimp.'' Thailand is one of the main exporters of shrimp to the United States. The report highlighted how companies in Thailand systematically use the lack of labor rights and weak labor law enforcement to exploit the mostly Burmese shrimp processing workers. The report uncovered major human rights abuses in the industry: unpaid wages, unsafe and unhealthy workplaces, child labor, forced labor, physical intimidation, violence and sexual abuse of Burmese migrant workers. Six years later, little progress has been made to clean up the industry. Reports continue to surface about human trafficking of migrant workers in the seafood processing sector in Thailand.[4] The Thai fishing industry has also received harsh criticism for the trafficking of migrant worker men, not only Burmese, but increasingly Cambodians and Rohingya refugees, onto fishing boats.[5] This was a major factor in the downgrading of Thailand in the 2014 TIP Report.[6] Just this year, the Guardian newspaper conducted a 6-month long investigation and found that a large number of migrant workers are bought and sold like slaves and held against their will on Thai fishing boats. The Guardian found that such forced labor plays an integral part in the production of shrimp sold in leading supermarkets around the world, including in the U.S. in stores such as Walmart, Costco, Carrefour, and Tesco.[7]

Despite the overwhelming evidence of a high vulnerability of migrant workers in Thailand to trafficking for forced labor and debt bondage, the Thai Government has done very little to address the problem, and in fact has implemented measures that may actually increase migrant workers vulnerability to labor trafficking.

It is an established norm in the anti-trafficking field that providing documentation and legal status to migrant workers reduces their vulnerability to human trafficking. The Thai Government, however, makes it difficult for migrant workers, and especially Burmese, to register and work legally in Thailand. As noted in a recent letter to Secretary of State Kerry from a global coalition of unions and human rights NGOs:

> A complicated, expensive registration process that requires nationality verification and lack of a refugee law leaves stateless people (mostly Rohingya from Burma), migrant workers, and refugees at the mercy of labor recruiters to arrange for the documents they need to live in Thailand legally. Even through the official state process, brokers are not licensed or regulated, workers are responsible for paying the majority of the registration costs, and there is no state mechanism through which to apply for asylum outside the camps on the Thai-Burma border. Thus, many workers find themselves in some form of debt bondage to brokers. . . . [R]egistration has

expired for more than 250,000 workers who often paid several times more than the official rate to register under the National Verification System 4 years ago. As their documents expire, and official directives of how they must renew them remain in flux, more and more migrant workers are going to find themselves in the country illegally and more vulnerable to trafficking.[8]

Migrant workers, ethnic minorities, and stateless persons in Thailand are the most vulnerable to human trafficking because they lack legal status. Lack of legal status, identity papers, and travel documents are major indicators for forced labor.

Moreover, the Thai Government continues to make it difficult for migrant workers to obtain permits to work legally in the country. Only employers can apply for work permits and the permit binds the worker to that employer. Work permits also are tied to registration documents, so even legally registered workers can be immediately deported for leaving an abusive employer. Workers often face physical abuse and other forms of retaliation if employers find out they complained to the authorities to seek better treatment or to transfer to another employer.[9]

Through our programs in vulnerable work sectors around the world, the Solidarity Center has seen firsthand how a democratically elected and independent union in a workplace can help prevent trafficking. And yet, the Thai Government has failed to amend its 1975 Labor Relations Act, which prohibits migrant workers from organizing labor unions, serving as leaders of a union, or participating in collective bargaining.

The recent military coup in Thailand also raises concerns. While it may be too early to tell how the current military government will respond to the human trafficking crisis, there have been reports of a crackdown on undocumented migrant workers, with hundreds of thousands of Cambodian workers fleeing over the border from Thailand back to Cambodia in early June 2014. We have seen in other countries where there is a forced mass exodus of migrant workers that workers face an increased vulnerability to exploitation as they cross the border back into their home country with few resources. (See example from Malaysia below). In recent days, the Thai and Cambodian Governments announced new measures to streamline the process for Cambodian migrant workers to return to Thailand to work legally, promising to lower fees to workers and shifting some recruitment costs to agencies.[10] While this sounds promising, whether it will actually help to reduce migrant workers vulnerability to forced labor and debt bondage remains to be seen.

Just last month, Thailand was the only government to vote against adoption of a new International Labor Organization (ILO) treaty on forced labor. I was a delegate on behalf of the AFL–CIO to the ILO Conference, which approved a key supplement to the 1930 Forced Labor Convention. The 2014 Forced Labor Protocol and Recommendation contain key provisions to help address the vulnerability of migrant workers to trafficking, such as the elimination of recruitment fees. Given Thailand's poor record on protecting migrant workers from human trafficking, its ''no'' vote was particularly troubling. Following the vote, after pressure from Thai labor unions and others, the Thai Government has indicated it will adopt the protocol. The United States and other governments should continue to exert pressure to ensure that the Thai Government ratifies the instrument.

Malaysia

Migrant workers in Malaysia face a similar situation as migrant workers in Thailand. Malaysia is one of the largest destination countries for migrant workers in Asia. There are approximately 2 million documented and 2 million undocumented migrant workers, including Indonesians, Nepalese, Filipinos, Indians, Bangladeshis, Sri Lankans, and increasingly Vietnamese, Cambodians, Burmese, and Laotians. These migrants comprise nearly 30 percent of the Malaysian workforce. While the Malaysian economy thrives on cheap migrant labor, foreign workers in sectors such as agriculture, construction, service, manufacturing, and domestic work often have their rights violated with little recourse under Malaysian laws, policies, and practices.

Despite the constant demand for cheap migrant labor, as well as an invariable influx of migrants, Malaysia does not have concrete policies and laws to protect migrant workers. The few existing policies protecting migrants are not enforced, or are enforced inconsistently, and tend to be short-term, temporary fixes. Malaysia has signed Memoranda of Understanding (MOUs) with several countries mentioned above, yet these agreements are often weak and difficult to enforce.

Migrant workers in Malaysia consistently face serious violations of internationally recognized labor and human rights. These violations include confiscation of passports, restrictions on movement, and deceit and fraud in wages (including nonpayment), forced labor, involuntary servitude, debt bondage and other forms of trafficking in persons. Physical and mental abuse, including sexual violence, is also a common phenomenon.

Debt bondage is a major problem for migrant workers in Malaysia. Employers increasingly rely on labor recruiters or employment agencies to recruit foreign workers. These recruiters/agencies charge high fees to migrant workers, often forcing workers to mortgage homes/land or to take out loans at exorbitant interest rates. Workers may end up in conditions of bondage, as they are unable to leave abusive employers because of the debt. The Malaysian Government and the origin governments have failed to adequately address this problem. Moreover, Malaysian employers shift additional costs to workers that are the employer's responsibility, and use other economic coercion tactics to deny migrant workers their rights. The U.S. Department of State explains this well:

> Many Malaysian recruitment companies, known as ''outsourcing companies,'' recruit workers from foreign countries. Contractor-based labor arrangements of this type—in which the worker may technically be employed by the recruiting company—create vulnerabilities for workers whose day-to-day employers generally are without legal responsibility for exploitative practices. In some cases, foreign workers' vulnerability to exploitation is heightened when employers neglect to obtain proper documentation for workers or employ workers in sectors other than that for which they were granted an employment visa. In addition, a complex system of recruitment and contracting fees, often deducted from workers' wages, makes workers vulnerable to debt bondage.⸺⸺11

Rule of law for migrant workers in Malaysia is weak. Labor laws exempt migrant workers, or are weakly enforced. Many laws do not comply with international labor standards. For example, Malaysia excludes certain categories of workers, like domestic workers, from the protection of its 1955 Employment Act. There is little support for trafficked workers to access justice. Migrant workers are often put in detention centers or deported even if they are victims of worker rights violations, including forced labor.

Although it is lawful for migrant workers to join unions in Malaysia, they are prohibited from holding leadership positions, and may be banned from joining a union if they are contract employees, which most migrant workers are. Moreover, many employment contracts for foreign workers contain provisions banning workers from joining labor unions. Origin governments, such as Vietnam, also prohibit workers from joining unions in Malaysia. Further, employers routinely fire and blacklist migrant workers for trying to form unions with impunity. Such restrictions on freedom of association further prevent migrant workers from accessing justice for worker rights violations because they cannot access grievance procedures, or use collective bargaining to gain rights in the workplace.

Union leaders and migrant workers activists in Asia have criticized the 2007 Malaysian Anti-Trafficking in Persons Act (ATIP) for merging smuggling and trafficking offenses, ''making trafficking victims more likely to be treated as undocumented migrants subject to immediate deportation, undermining government efforts to counter trafficking.'' 12

Similar to the Thai Government, the Malaysian Government has actually implemented policies recently that are increasing migrant workers vulnerability to forced labor rather than decreasing it. For example, a Malaysian Government policy implemented in January 2013 places the burden of paying immigration and employment authorization fees on foreign workers, rather than on employers, increasing the risk of debt bondage. Moreover, the Malaysian Government periodically implements crackdowns on undocumented migrants, most recently in January 2014, where they conducted massive operations to detain and deport hundreds of thousands of migrant workers. However, the Malaysian Government does not have adequate screening procedures to ensure that trafficking victims are not also detained and deported. In addition, the deportations often involve leaving migrant workers literally just over the border in Indonesia without any resources or support. Indonesian NGOs report that these migrant workers are then vulnerable to traffickers who promise them new jobs or assistance in getting home.

Finally, the Malaysian Trade Union Congress (MTUC), which is active on the promotion of migrant worker rights and the eradication of labor trafficking, notes that the Malaysian Government has been blocking the completion of the ASEAN Framework Instrument on the Protection and Promotion of Human Rights, which migrant worker rights activists have been pushing for since 2007.

Cambodia

Unlike Thailand and Malaysia, Cambodia is primarily an origin country for migrant workers traveling mostly within the ASEAN region (often to Thailand and Malaysia). Cambodian men, women, and children have been subjected to forced labor, domestic servitude, and debt bondage, in sectors such as fishing, agriculture, manufacturing, and domestic work.

Similar to the situation of its neighbors, recruitment agencies play a major role in the trafficking of Cambodian workers. Agencies, along with corrupt local government officials, falsify legal identification documents to facilitate the illegal migration of children. Labor recruiters also charge exorbitant fees to migrant workers. A Solidarity Center Cambodian partner NGO cited fees as high as $600, which may be 1 year's salary for a low-wage migrant worker. Such fees often push Cambodian migrant workers into debt bondage. Corrupt Cambodian officials have also been implicated in cooperating with labor recruiters to facilitate the transport of victims across the border into Thailand.[13]

The Cambodian Government's response to labor recruiter violations has been weak, and rife with corruption. For example, a local Cambodian newspaper reported:

> [T]he appointment of General Sok Phal to head the Interior Ministry's newly formed department to monitor migrant workers has raised concerns over his close familial connection to a labor recruitment industry fraught with human rights abuses. Gen. Phal's sister, Ung Seang Rithy, is the owner of one of the biggest labor recruitment agencies sending Cambodian workers overseas . . . the Ung Rithy Group, which has been named by rights groups as a serial abuser of Cambodian migrant workers. Ms. Seang Rithy is also president of the Association of Cambodian Recruitment Agencies . . . "When I heard this news, I was concerned about the close relationships between high-ranking people in the government and in recruitment agencies," said Moeun Tola, head of the labor program at the Community Legal Education Center. "Since the Labor Ministry failed to properly manage and monitor [migrant workers], labor recruitment basically became human trafficking," Mr. Tola said. "The Ministry of Interior will now take on much more of the work, meaning Sok Phal will have even more influence than before." . . .[14]

In response to harsh media reports of Cambodian women and girls being trafficked into domestic servitude in Malaysia,[15] the Cambodian Government instituted a ban on the migration of women to Malaysia for domestic work. The Cambodian Government, however, lacks the infrastructure, capacity, and resources to manage labor migration and there are reports that Cambodian women and girls continue to migrate to Malaysia through even more insecure channels and methods, increasing their vulnerability to trafficking. The Cambodian Ministry of Labor is currently finalizing a draft MOU with its Malaysian counterpart to facilitate the migration of domestic workers once again from Cambodia to Malaysia. Without effective enforcement measures, however, activists are skeptical that the MOU will protect Cambodian domestic workers. Cambodian men have also been a large percentage of the victims of forced labor described above on Thai fishing boats.

The Cambodian Government promotes labor migration as a way to increase national revenue (through remittances) and address high unemployment in the country. Yet the government fails to monitor the recruitment process, enforce labor recruiter regulations, and support Cambodian workers in destination countries. The government has not created the structures or infrastructure to support Cambodian workers abroad. It negotiates weak agreements with destination countries (the MOU with Malaysia in relation to domestic workers is a prime example). Cambodian Embassies abroad are ill-equipped to deal with the large numbers of exploited and trafficked Cambodian workers. There is very little accountability for corruption.

ASEAN

The planned ASEAN Economic Community (AEC), currently being developed by the 10 Association of Southeast Asian Nations (ASEAN) member states, will include initiatives related to labor mobility in the region. The proposed labor mobility negates the whole concept of "migrant workers" at least for citizens of member states, though high-skilled workers will have easier mobility than low-wage workers. The ASEAN labor mobility initiatives, however, are being developed without any accompanying safeguards or labor rights standards to ensure that migrant workers will be protected. Migrant worker rights activists in the region have serious concerns that without the proper infrastructure in place, including strong regulations, migrant workers' vulnerability to forced labor and human trafficking will likely increase. Cambodian labor rights activists are particularly concerned for Cambodian workers, who will be a large percentage of the low-wage workers leaving their homes to travel to other ASEAN countries (like Malaysia and Thailand) to work in the most dangerous jobs, and in jobs the most rife for exploitation.

Lack of investigations, prosecutions, and convictions for forced labor (linked to corruption, complacency and even complicity of government officials in labor trafficking)

Systematic abuse of migrant workers, rising to the level of forced labor and human trafficking, goes virtually unpunished throughout Asia. The 2014 TIP Report country narratives for Thailand, Malaysia, and Cambodia provide examples of these governments' reluctance to hold employers accountable for trafficking in their workplaces. Even in the rare cases when labor trafficking is identified and charges brought, the labor recruiter is blamed and not the employer who also perpetrates the exploitation. This lack of political will translates into pathetically few cases of human trafficking for forced labor or other forms of severe labor exploitation being prosecuted in the region. When cases are prosecuted, they often result in small fines and no jail time for the perpetrators—barely a deterrent for exploitative employers. Or cases get put on hold for years while perpetrators are out on bail.

While public awareness campaigns and education for at-risk groups are important tools for prevention, one of the key ways to prevent forced labor is to create an enabling environment through the rule of law that promotes transparency and accountability. Increasing prosecutions and convictions, and imposing harsh penalties (including long jail time and economic restitution) may be an even more effective prevention tool.

As mentioned above, corrupt officials in Thailand, Malaysia, and Cambodia are part of the problem. For example, Thai Government officials have been implicated in the trafficking of Rohingya refugees on Thai fishing boats. Cambodian officials have been tied directly to working with labor recruiters to traffic workers over the border to Thailand, and Malaysian immigration officials have been linked to facilitating the transportation of trafficking victims. Human Rights Watch has reported that abuses of Cambodian migrant domestic workers by employers and recruiters "went unchecked due to connections between recruitment agencies and highly placed officials." [16]

Moreover, whistleblowers, in the form of trade union or NGO activists, journalists, and migrant workers, have been retaliated against by all three governments for raising issues of forced labor and corruption linked to human trafficking. For example, late last year, Thai authorities charged two journalists with defamation for writing and publishing a report alleging that members of the Thai navy were involved in trafficking captured migrants from Burma. This not only raises concerns about the freedom of the press, but also concerns of how the Thai military will respond to trafficking abuses now that it is in charge of the government.

The Solidarity Center sees the low levels of forced labor prosecutions, lack of political will and impunity as evidence of these governments' absolute disregard of forced labor as a serious issue. Labor migration is seen as a profitmaking mechanism, for employers, owners of recruitment agencies, and government officials, and human trafficking as just an unfortunate consequence.

The lack of economic pressure by governments and businesses to eliminate forced labor and other forms of labor trafficking in the supply chains of products exported to the United States and other global destinations

Clearly, Thailand, Malaysia and Cambodia are important bilateral partners for the United States. They are also important trade partners. Malaysia is part of the Trans-Pacific Partnership (TPP) negotiations with the United States and 10 other countries. The U.S. and Cambodia negotiated the Trade and Investment Framework Agreement (TIFA) in 2006, which "facilitates and promotes greater trade and investment of the two countries and provides a forum to address bilateral trade and investment issues." [17] Thailand is one of the largest exporters of seafood to the United States. The AFL–CIO has filed a petition to suspend Generalized System of Preferences (GSP) status for Thailand with the U.S. Trade Representative (USTR). The AFL–CIO has called for a suspension of GSP as a way to incentivize the Thai Government to effectively address forced labor and human trafficking, and other labor rights abuses of migrant and Thai workers. The U.S. is a major market for Malaysian and Cambodian ready-made garments. Given the significant problem of trafficking of migrant workers along the supply chains in these and other export sectors, it is likely the U.S. Government is allowing imports of products made with forced labor into the United States.

When the Solidarity Center issued its True Cost of Shrimp report in 2008, we were immediately attacked by Thai shrimp producers and industry associations, who all claimed that they had good labor practices and clean supply chains. The companies also made promises to be transparent and institute measures to ensure that there was no forced labor in fishing and seafood production in Thailand. Yet every year since, the media, unions, and NGOs have provided strong evidence of forced labor in the industry. When the State Department ranked Thailand on Tier 3 last month, the Thai fishing industry again claimed the allegations were outrageous.[18] The industry representatives can make these false claims because they know that they likely will not be held accountable by the Thai Government or anyone else.

U.S. multinationals may be complicit in this. As mentioned earlier, Thailand is one of the largest importers of shrimp to the U.S.; resulting in Thai shrimp ending up in the freezers of major retailers here. As buyers of Thai processed seafood, these U.S. companies have not done enough to prove to consumers that their supply chains are not tainted with forced labor.

Again, public awareness campaigns and education for at-risk groups are important tools for prevention; but in and of themselves they will not eradicate trafficking for forced labor. Together with increased prosecutions and convictions, one of the most effective prevention tools that governments and businesses have is economic pressure. Governments should impose trade restrictions or penalties on products made with forced labor, and multinational corporations should exert their significant power as buyers to hold suppliers accountable to supply chains free of forced labor.

In general, it is difficult to quantify the exact number of forced labor victims in global supply chains but, as those supply chains reach down to smaller and smaller suppliers, the chances increase that the labor force includes trafficked people.

- When employers (buyers and multinational corporations) demand cheap or unrealistic pricing structures, severe labor abuses, including forced labor, often will result in their supply chains.
- Similarly, when employers contract out or hire unregulated subcontracted suppliers, they should not be surprised to find that they have trafficking victims in their production lines.
- When employers refuse to enforce or claim that it is too difficult to monitor adherence to core labor standards in their supply chains, the probability that they will find forced labor, debt bondage, and other severe forms of labor exploitation increases.

The pricing structure as a cause of human trafficking cannot be overemphasized, as this is an underlying factor that employers, business, corporations and consumers can all address. As described in the Solidarity Center's report, ''The True Cost of Shrimp'':

> As a commodity, the price of shrimp fluctuates according to supply and demand, and price pressure is significant all along the supply chain. Retailers, sensitive to the risk involved with importing fresh food, press import companies for faster distribution, acceptable quality, and the lowest prices. Importers, aware that market fluctuations can affect prices, leverage their bulk purchasing power to demand speedy delivery from producers. Trapped between producers and importers are labor-intensive shrimp factories. Often, the factories' response to price pressure is to squeeze wages, neglect workplace health and safety regulations, and cut other corners that leave shrimp workers bearing the social cost of affordable shrimp.[19]

And yet, Thai shrimp continues to be found in major U.S. retail markets. Similar concerns may be raised on the potential of forced labor in the supply chains of products exported from Malaysia and Cambodia.

The U.S. Government must do more to ensure that U.S. corporations are held accountable for their practices abroad. And we must increase government scrutiny of imports and exports to ensure goods made by forced labor are not allowed in the U.S. marketplace. The 1930 Tariff Act prohibits the importation of goods into the U.S. made with forced or child labor. This law however is rarely enforced as the ''consumptive demand exception'' weakens it. As required by the 2005 TVPRA, the U.S. Department of Labor ''maintains a list of goods and their source countries which it has reason to believe are produced by child labor or forced labor in violation of international standards.''[20] Even though many of the goods on the list are produced for export by the identified countries, the list has not been used to enforce the Tariff Act.

After the publication of the Solidarity Center's "True Cost of Shrimp" report, Senator Harkin asked the Department of Homeland Security (DHS) to investigate. U.S. Immigration and Customs Enforcement (ICE) investigators admitted to the Solidarity Center that they knew that their investigation would not find forced labor in the Thai seafood sector because the investigation process is flawed. Currently, ICE must notify foreign governments of their intent to inspect workplaces that export products to the United States. Such notification results in the "cleansing" of these workplaces to remove any signs of trafficking or forced labor. Moreover, U.S. law does not allow evidence collected by unions, the media or nongovernmental sources to be the basis for restricting the importation of products made by trafficked or forced labor. This must be reformed. The DHS must review and rework the role of ICE in overseas inspections.

Multinational corporations' codes of conduct have failed to curtail trafficking practices in many sectors, including garment/textile, agriculture, and seafood processing. There is no easy solution to this problem, but we know that a key deterrent is the ability of unions and labor rights organizations to shine a light on these practices through on-the-ground investigations. We believe it is important that Congress and the administration support such monitoring efforts and the efforts of workers to monitor their own workplaces. Ultimately, workers and trade unions must be empowered to monitor supply chains because history shows that abuses in the workplace only end when workers have the power to ensure that their rights in ILO conventions and national laws are respected.

RECOMMENDATIONS FOR INITIATIVES TO COMBAT TRAFFICKING FOR LABOR EXPLOITATION IN THE EAST ASIA REGION

"End Worker Exploitation, End Human Trafficking." This simple slogan captures one of the most critical solutions to ending human trafficking in Thailand, Malaysia, and Cambodia as migrant worker exploitation is a major factor in forced labor in the region.

Key initiatives to combat trafficking for labor exploitation in the region should include:

1. Using trade agreements to prevent forced labor (economic pressure)

a. Congress, the administration, and other governments should ensure that bilateral and multilateral trade agreements (like the TPP) contain labor standards and protections as a preventative measure, ensuring they are applied to all workers, including migrants. Labor standards in trade agreements should include the same enforcement and dispute resolution mechanisms as other provisions like intellectual property rights, and not be relegated to secondary status.

b. Congress should encourage and support the United States Trade Representative (USTR) to suspend GSP and other trade preferences for any country that does not effectively address forced labor. Given the clear evidence of forced labor of migrant workers in Thailand, once Congress reauthorizes the GSP program, the USTR should give serious consideration to the AFL–CIO's petition to suspend Thailand's GSP status. Economic pressure is key to eradicating forced labor.

Prevention through regulation of labor recruiters

a. Congress and other governments should strictly regulate labor recruiters and employment agencies. Specifically, eliminate worker recruitment fees and shift costs back to the employer. Workers should not be required to pay any fees associated with recruitment, the migration process, or placement. Employers must be held liable for the abuses of labor recruiters they hire. In addition, workers must have a way to ensure that a recruiter is legitimate and licensed.

b. To that end, the Senate passed Subtitle F: Prevention of Trafficking in Persons and Abuses Involving Workers Recruited Abroad and similar provisions in Subtitle I as part of S. 744 (Immigration Reform) in 2013 is a significant step forward in addressing #15 above. In the House of Representatives, H.R. 3344, introduced last year by Chairman Ed Royce, is modeled after Subtitle F, and has bipartisan support with over 70 cosponsors. The Senate and the House of Representatives should make efforts at the earliest possible time to pass such legislation to end fraud in our nonimmigrant visa programs and prevent trafficking in the labor recruitment system. Not only will such a law help to protect migrant workers in the U.S.; but, it will also serve as a powerful model for other countries, such as Thailand, Malaysia, and Cambodia, which need to pass and enforce similar laws and policies.

c. Thailand, Malaysia and Cambodia must specifically adopt measures to de-link government officials from recruitment agencies, including measures to address possible conflicts of interest. High level prosecutions of corrupt government officials and owners of labor recruitment agencies would also send a powerful message.

3. Safe Migration

Congress and the administration (J/TIP, DRL, DOL, DOJ) should emphasize safer migration processes for workers. Immigration policies should emphasize ways to make workers safer during the migration process, and reflect economic reality. For Thailand and Malaysia, this means ending operations that result in mass deportations of undocumented migrant workers, without effective measures in place to identify and support trafficking victims. It also means ensuring that deported workers are provided with a safe passage home. Finally, Thailand and Malaysia should amend their laws and policies to make it easier for migrant workers to obtain valid work permits and residency documents at little or no cost, in streamlined processes.

4. The rule of law (prosecutions and accountability)

a. Governments should increase the number of prosecutions and convictions for forced labor. For Thailand, Malaysia, and Cambodia, this means training police and prosecutors to better investigate and prosecute forced labor cases; and protecting police and other law enforcement officials from retaliation by powerful employers, businessowners or high-level government officials for bringing cases forward.

b. Penalize abusive workplaces. Strengthen enforcement and penalties against employers who are found to have trafficked workers or to companies who have bought products or raw materials made by forced labor. This means prosecuting employers and imposing stiff penalties. Employers must be held accountable for the abuses of their subcontractors, including labor recruiters, and for abuses in their supply chains.

5. The rule of law (creating an enabling environment)

a. Congress, the administration, governments in the region, and multinational corporations should ensure freedom of association, the right to organize, join trade unions and collectively bargain for all workers, regardless of status or nationality, in both origin and destination countries, and as an essential component of ASEAN economic integration.

b. For Thailand and Malaysia, the freedom of association must be assured in practice and not just law. This means strict penalties for employers who fire, blacklist, or retaliate against migrant workers who try to organize; and reform of laws that prohibit migrant workers from joining or holding leadership positions in unions, and from participating in collective bargaining.

c. Thailand, Malaysia and Cambodia should reform their labor and other laws to include and protect migrant and domestic workers. All workers—whether national or foreign, documented or undocumented—must have equal protection under the law, and receive full protection of the laws. In addition, governments and employers must recognize and enforce all ILO core labor standards, including the freedom of association and right to organize.

d. Congress and the Departments of State and Labor should promote the ratification and implementation of ILO Convention 189 on Decent Work for Domestic Workers, and the ILO Protocol of 2014 to the Forced Labor Convention, 1930 and its accompanying Recommendation.

e. Congress, the administration, and governments in the region should give equal attention not only to passing better laws, but also implementing, monitoring, and enforcing those laws. To do so, governments must enhance the role of labor inspectors. Labor inspectors must be engaged in and be an integral part of law enforcement initiatives to combat human trafficking. In particular, labor inspectors must be given special training to recognize the signs of human trafficking in a workplace, including debt bondage and other forms of economic coercion that result in human trafficking, and to identify victims. Governments must also ensure that there are sufficient numbers of labor inspectors, and that they have the responsibility to inspect all workplaces—including those with high percentages of migrant workers.

f. Congress and the Thai, Malaysian and Cambodian Governments must pass national whistleblower protection laws regarding trafficked workers. Also, companies should ensure that there are such protections in company policy all along the supply chain, and advocate to governments for such protections for workers.

6. Preventing the importation of goods made with forced labor

a. DHS should increase scrutiny of imports and exports to ensure goods made by trafficked or forced labor are not allowed in the U.S. marketplace. This includes reviewing and re-working the role of ICE in overseas inspections. The Senate may consider holding a hearing on this issue.

b. Congress should amend the Tariff Act of 1930 to remove the ''consumptive demand exception.'' The demand loophole ''renders the ban almost useless, since courts have ruled that U.S. Customs cannot block any product unless the U.S.

makes enough of it to meet 100 percent of domestic needs . . . The 1930 provision is unsuited to a globalized 21st-century economy that gives importers a wide choice of suppliers. As the dominant force in this new era, the U.S. has an obligation to set the example.'' [21] Congress and the administration should also amend U.S. law and policy to allow evidence collected by unions or nongovernmental sources to be the basis for restricting the importation of products made by forced labor.

c. As an immediate measure to implement #11 and #12, DHS and Congress should review the importation of Thai seafood under the 1930 Tariff Act.

7. Supply chain accountability

a. Congress should increase pressure on companies to map their supply chains and make such information public. Companies argue that it is too difficult or expensive to completely map their supply chains. If NGOs and the media can do it, however, companies can too. There needs to be a change in business practices.

b. To that end, Congress should pass supply chain transparency legislation, similar to H.R. 4842, the Business Supply Chain Transparency on Trafficking and Slavery Act of 2014, which was introduced on a bipartisan basis by Representatives Maloney and Smith on June 11, 2014. Such legislation would require companies to report annually to the SEC and on their Web sites what measures they have taken to address forced labor, human trafficking, and the worst forms of child labor within their business operations, including supply chains and labor management, in a way that is consistent with the obligations of businesses as outlined by the U.N. Guiding Principles on Human Rights. While such legislation would purely be a transparency measure, we see it as a first step in ensuring forced labor-free supply chains.

c. As an effective way to monitor supply chains for trafficking and forced labor, Congress, the administration, other governments, and businesses should promote freedom of association and the right to organize, worker agency and worker representation, over codes of conduct and third party monitoring. The Bangladesh Accord on Fire and Building Safety and Coalition of Immokalee Workers' Fair Food Program are promising models of how to do this.

8. U.S. Government Bilateral and Multilateral Support

a. Congress and the administration should provide support to origin countries (like Cambodia, Indonesia and Bangladesh) to negotiate multilateral agreements with more powerful destination countries to level the playing field for migrant workers. Because of unequal bargaining power, and the desire of developing origin countries for remittances and employment abroad for their citizens, bilateral agreements are often weak, and provide few worker rights protections. Multilateral agreements may provide more avenues for labor standards.

b. Congress should authorize and appropriate sufficient long-term resources to the Department of State's Bureau of Democracy, Human Rights and Labor (DRL) and J/TIP, as well as the Department of Labor-International Labor Office (ILAB) to support government efforts in Thailand, Malaysia, and Cambodia, and in other high-risk countries around the world, in their efforts to combat forced labor and other forms of trafficking for labor exploitation. All three agencies have an important role to play in this effort to provide technical assistance to governments and moral and financial support for civil society (including Solidarity Center long-term local partners) in all three countries to enhance monitoring and implementation of anti-trafficking capacity building programs.

c. Congress should continue to call for the Department of State to strengthen the labor reporting function in its Embassies abroad. The Cambodian Government should also assign, and properly train, labor attachés in Embassies abroad where there are large numbers of Cambodian migrant workers.

9. Victim Protection

a. Promote better protection measures for victims. For Thailand and Malaysia, this means training government officials to recognize and identify victims of forced labor and other forms of labor trafficking, and not detain or deport them as undocumented migrants.

b. Provide compensation to victims, including payment of withheld or back wages.

Thank you, again, for the opportunity to testify and for your help to combat labor trafficking in the East Asia and Pacific region. I welcome your questions.

End Notes

[1] The term ''migrant worker'' is the internationally accepted term for a person who migrates for employment, whether temporary, seasonal, or permanent. In the United States, in everyday language, ''migrant worker'' may refer to a seasonal or temporary worker, and ''immigrant worker'' refers to someone who migrates for work on a more permanent basis, or who has residency

rights. I will use the term "migrant worker" in my testimony to refer to all workers who migrate for work, regardless of their status or length of stay in the destination country.

[2] Office of Inspections, Inspection of the Office to Monitor & Combat Trafficking in Persons, Report Number ISP–I–12–37 (June 2012).

[3] There were a few rankings in the 2014 TIP Report that advocates believe were based on political considerations—India and the Dominican Republic to name two; however, we can save that discussion for another hearing.

[4] See for example: "Trafficked into Slavery on Thai Trawlers to Catch Food for Prawns," The Guardian, June 10, 2014.

[5] See "Special Report: "Thailand Secretly Supplies Myanmar Refugees to Trafficking Rings," Reuters, December 4, 2014.

[6] http://www.state.gov/j/tip/rls/tiprpt/countries/2014/226832.htm.

[7] See "Revealed: Asian Slave Labour Producing Prawns for Supermarkets in U.S., U.K.," The Guardian, June 10, 2014. See also "Thailand's seafood industry: a case of state-sanctioned slavery?" The Guardian, June 10, 2014.

[8] "Letter to Secretary of State John Kerry Regarding Human Trafficking in Thailand," May 9, 2014.

[9] "Letter to Secretary of State John Kerry Regarding Human Trafficking in Thailand," May 9, 2014.

[10] See "King Grants Pardon to Thai Activist Veera", The Cambodia Daily, July 2, 2014.

[11] http://www.state.gov/j/tip/rls/tiprpt/countries/2014/226770.htm

[12] "More Bold Actions Need to be Done to Address Trafficking in Persons in Malaysia," Statement by José Sonny G. Matula, National President, Federation of Free Workers-Philippines, to the 2014 International Labor Conference, June 2014.

[13] See Trafficking in Persons Report 2014.

[14] "Concern over Migration Chief's Family Connections," The Cambodia Daily, April 24, 2014.

[15] See, for example, "Cambodia: Trafficking Domestic Workers to Malaysia," IRIN, March 17, 2011.

[16] "'They Deceived Us at Every Step.' Abuse of Cambodian Domestic Workers Migrating to Malaysia," Human Rights Watch, 2011.

[17] http://www.ustr.gov/tpp.

[18] "Fishery Invites Supply Chain Inspection," The Nation, June 25, 2014.

[19] The True Cost of Shrimp, Solidarity Center, 2008, p. 11.

[20] http://www.dol.gov/ilab/reports/child-labor/list-of-goods/.

[21] "U.S. Can Help End Child Labor by Amending 1930 Tariff Act: View," Bloomberg View, January 2, 2012.

Senator CARDIN. Thank you very much.

Mr. Eaves.

STATEMENT OF JESSE EAVES, SENIOR POLICY ADVISOR FOR CHILD PROTECTION, WORLD VISION, WASHINGTON, DC

Mr. EAVES. Thank you so much, Mr. Chairman, for convening this incredibly important hearing and for inviting us to testify today.

Both you and Senator Rubio are leaders in the fight against forced labor, human trafficking, and modern-day slavery. And, thanks to your tireless efforts, America remains a global leader in combating these and other crucial issues that endanger and impact children around the world. And this hearing really is an important opportunity to shine a light on what is happening in East Asia and discuss how the United States can strengthen its role as a partner in the region.

World Vision is a Christian relief, development, and advocacy organization that focuses on serving millions of children and families around the world, in about 100 countries. Our 45,000 employees are dedicated to working with children, families, and their communities to really tackle the root causes of poverty and injustice.

We have been asked to testify about our experience in preventing and responding to forced labor and human trafficking in East Asia. And East Asian countries are a vital and increasingly influential component to the global economy, yet the region is also home to large pockets of the poorest and most vulnerable people on Earth. The nature of the global marketplace is producing many opportunities to make money in a few East Asian nations, but it is also creating more ways to exploit a person for their labor. The opportunity is now and the tools are available to make U.S. engagement and funding more coordinated, effective, and efficient in tackling this vulnerability. So, together with partners in East Asia, we can ensure that the region's growth is built on the strengths of its people and not on their backs, through bondage.

So, in other countries, including America, you know, forced labor and human trafficking take on many forms, as they do in East Asia, so we see children exploited as child soldiers, working in brickkilns, in the construction industry, the fishing industry, and forced to be domestic servants. And, as Neha mentioned, it is nearly impossible to address the issue of forced labor and human trafficking in the region without talking about migration.

My written testimony contains the full account of Min Min, a Burmese boy who was sold to an Indonesian fishing vessel and spent 9 years as a slave at sea. Cases like these have led World Vision to spend a great deal of effort educating communities, especially children aged 15 through 17—that is the age where they are most likely to go seek a job—we educate them on the dangers of risky migration and the proactive steps that they can take to prevent themselves from becoming victims.

So, for instance, throughout Southeast Asia, we provide this booklet, called ''The Smart Navigator Booklet.'' It is small, easy to understand; it covers what human trafficking is like; and it is provided in local languages. It provides a checklist for ensuring safe travel, and even includes basic information, like how to make an international phone call. So, these simple, yet effective, steps come from having seen so many stories like Min Min's, when migrating to earn money goes wrong.

So, the details of the dangers of unsafe migration and trafficking and countless other insights fill the pages of the U.S. State Department's TIP Report. And that reports serves as an invaluable tool in the U.S. diplomatic toolbox to combat human trafficking. And the findings and recommendations listed in the country narratives often inform the development of governments' laws and national action plans to combat trafficking. So, these plans provide a guide for what governments need to do in order to strengthen their efforts, and provides NGOs like World Vision with a roadmap that shows what a government's priorities are in this area. So, these action plans create an opening for us to work alongside governments to accomplish their goals.

And, just as an aside, it is critical to point out that governments cannot make progress alone, and there is no single intervention or effort that can defeat the use of forced labor and human trafficking in the long term. So, World Vision programs have been most successful when we have taken a multifaceted, multisector approach to combating exploitation.

So, for example, in a project in Cambodia funded by the U.S. Department of Labor, World Vision reaches 28,000 children who have worked in the fishing industry, in agriculture, domestic servitude, and other sectors. The program focuses on protection, education, household income, access to credit, empowerment of local communities, and the list goes on.

World Vision also focuses on another key factor that most people take for granted, which is birth registration. Human traffickers pursue individuals who are vulnerable and powerless. And without a birth certificate, children are an especially easy target. And, Senator Rubio, I want to thank you, in particular, for the work you have done recently in this area.

The U.S. Government has multiple options for partnering with East Asian governments. In addition to the diplomatic tool that is the TIP Report, the U.S. Government has tools to build on the recommendations that the TIP Report provides, with strategic, multisector, bilateral relationships in focus countries. I can refer you to my written testimony for a full list that includes USAID's counter-trafficking-in-persons policy, the action plan for children in adversity, and the key provisions of the Child Protection Compact Act which both of you supported in the 2013 reauthorization of the Trafficking Victims Protection Act. I thank you again for that support.

These tools allow for constructive and coordinated bilateral partnerships that will enable these countries to develop and expand their systems of prevention, protection, and prosecution, and ideally address many of the root causes of trafficking in the region. So, you all, in Congress, have given the administration good tools, and it is critical that we continue to work together so these tools are not left to rust in the toolbox.

So, we thank you again for holding this hearing and for all the work that you both continue to do to fight forced labor and human trafficking. We are committed to working with you all and with the subcommittee on these critical issues. And I look forward to your questions.

Thank you.

[The prepared statement of Mr. Eaves follows:]

PREPARED STATEMENT OF JESSE EAVES

Thank you, Mr. Chairman, for convening this important hearing and inviting World Vision to testify. You and Senator Rubio are leaders in the fight against forced labor, human trafficking, and modern day slavery. We are especially grateful that you have championed programs for the protection of vulnerable children. Children around the world are alive, and contributing to their communities and countries, because of these programs. Your efforts have led to an increased U.S. focus on displaced children, orphans, children affected by armed conflict, and children trafficked for sex or labor. Thanks to your tireless efforts, America remains a global leader in combating these and other critical issues that impact and endanger children. This hearing is an opportunity to shine a light on what is happening in East Asia and the Pacific and discuss how the U.S. can strengthen its leadership role.

World Vision is a Christian relief, development, and advocacy organization serving millions of children and families in nearly 100 countries. Our 45,000 employees are dedicated to working with children, families, and their communities to tackle the root causes of poverty and injustice. This work includes emergency relief and preparedness for people impacted by natural disasters and armed conflict; long-term economic development; preventing and responding to abuse, neglect, exploitation, and violence against children; mobilizing children, youth and local communities to hold their governments accountable; and advocating for effective systems, laws, and policies that provide a safety net and protection for vulnerable populations where the social fabric is especially weak.

World Vision U.S. has more than 1 million private donors in every state and congressional district, partners with over 16,000 churches in the United States, and works with corporations and foundations. We are part of the global federation of World Vision International, which last year implemented more than $2.6 billion in programming to help children and communities through international relief, development, and advocacy assistance. Although private donors support much of our work, the U.S. Government is an invaluable partner. We leverage this partnership to reach many more children at risk and ensure that the precious resources of the

American taxpayer are prudently used to promote and protect the well-being of children and communities abroad.

World Vision has been asked to testify about our experience preventing and responding to forced labor and human trafficking in East Asia. Our testimony will focus on the U.S. role in combating forced labor and human trafficking in the region; the importance of the State Department's Trafficking in Persons Report in addressing human trafficking in the region; what the 2014 tier placements in the Trafficking in Persons Report mean for the listed countries and the U.S.; and the impact of programs (U.S. funded and non-U.S. funded) and funding that aim to prevent these crimes. East Asian countries are a vital and increasingly influential component to the global economy. Yet the region is also home to large pockets of the poorest and most vulnerable people on Earth. The opportunity is now, and tools are available, to make U.S. engagement and funding more coordinated, effective, and efficient. Together with partners in East Asia, we can ensure that the region's growth is built on the strengths of the people, not on their backs through bondage.

According to the International Labor Organization, forced labor and human trafficking is a $150 billion industry. Most media and governmental attention to human trafficking focuses on sex trafficking. However, labor trafficking ensnares more people and makes more money. This is true in East Asian countries like Cambodia, Laos, Myanmar, the Philippines, Thailand, and Vietnam.

As in other countries, including America, forced labor and human trafficking take on many forms in East Asia. We see children exploited as child soldiers, working in brick kilns, agriculture, construction, the fishing industry, and forced to be domestic servants. All of these countries have laws that address human trafficking and fight labor exploitation to varying degrees. As in other countries—including America—there is a disconnect between national laws on forced labor and human trafficking and local level implementation and awareness of those laws. In fact, most laws focus on sex trafficking and often leave labor trafficking as a neglected priority at the national and local level. As a result, the level of impunity is high and the chances of justice for survivors is often low. There is often little reason for employers and traffickers to clean up their act. Furthermore, there are multiple root causes for forced labor and trafficking including household income levels, lack of education, issues of land tenure, and an increasing demand for cheap, unskilled labor. Every story is different. They still all point to how governments, civil society, and communities can do better to end modern day slavery.

In East Asia, migration, within and outside a country's border, is a common factor for many of the children whom we work with. The nature of the global market place is producing many opportunities to make money in a few East Asian nations but is also creating more ways to exploit a person for their labor. What's more, economic growth in countries like Thailand, Indonesia, and Malaysia has not been matched in countries like Myanmar, Laos, and Vietnam. This creates a strong demand for low-skilled labor that cannot be met by the local population. As a result, a steady supply of cheap, and often exploitable, labor moves from one country to another or from rural areas to urban centers. It is nearly impossible to address the issue of forced labor and human trafficking in the region without talking about migration. We have seen families in communities where we work in Vietnam, Cambodia, and the Philippines torn apart by high amounts of debt that they take on to pay the fees that unscrupulous employment agencies often require to secure a job abroad. These jobs are often not what was promised and can lead to the dark hole of debt bondage. Understanding and addressing the push and pull factors toward unsafe migration are critical to preventing and responding to vulnerability.

Let me share the story of Min Min, who has benefited from one of our programs in Myanmar. As the eldest son from a poor family in Myanmar, Min Min felt the pressure to help his family earn money and survive. He befriended a man who came to his village and told him he could get work in Thailand. When Min Min arrived in Thailand by boat, he was immediately sold to an Indonesian fishing vessel. He describes his ordeal as nothing short of hell. He was forced to work all night and most of the day for 7 days a week. He says he watched his captures torture or kill anyone who tried to escape. For 9 years, Min Min toiled on the boat until finally, one night, desperate to escape, he slipped off the boat and swam to shore. He found himself in Indonesia with no food, shoes, nor clothes. He made it to a small village but with no visa or identity documents there was little that the villagers could do for him. Min Min was finally able to call his family who contacted World Vision. We worked with the Myanmar Government to get him back home and end his ordeal. World Vision's End Trafficking in Persons Program (ETIP) provides direct assistance to trafficking survivors like Min Min to fully recover from the trafficking harm and reintegrate into life in society.

Min min's story illustrates where so much can go wrong and what can be done to help prepare migrants for what they might face when they leave home to work. In Myanmar, Vietnam, and Laos, we've worked with scores of children who were promised a job either in another city or another country only to find a situation that was nothing like they were promised and were forced into a situation where they are denied even the most basic human dignity. Cases like these have led World Vision to spend a great deal of effort educating communities and especially children aged 15–17 (those most likely to take a job) on the dangers of risky migration and the proactive steps they can take to prevent themselves from becoming victims. Throughout Southeast Asia, World Vision runs youth clubs that follow a toolkit composed of safe migration and trafficking prevention skills and information. Youth participants receive a pocket guide in local languages called the ''Smart Navigator Booklet,'' developed by World Vision's ETIP Program. This small, easy to understand booklet covers what human trafficking is; provides checklists for ensuring safe travel including keeping all identification documents with you; includes warnings against borrowing money or placing yourself in debt to your employer; and what to do if you think you've been trafficked including anti-trafficking hotlines in every country in East Asia. It even includes basic instructions on how to make an international phone call. These simple, yet effective, steps come from having seen so many stories like Min Min's when migrating to earn money goes wrong.

None of what is mentioned above should be considered new. Details about the dangers of unsafe migration and trafficking, and countless other insights, fill the pages of the U.S. State Department's annual Trafficking in Persons (TIP) Report. The TIP Report serves as an invaluable tool in the U.S. diplomatic toolbox to combat human trafficking. The report is a critical resource to organizations like World Vision and (though they may be loath to admit it) governments around the world. Whether country governments denounce the TIP Report, and bristle or rejoice in their rankings, the TIP Report is a key driver for national change. The findings and recommendations listed in country narratives often inform the development of governments' laws and National Action Plans (NAP) to combat trafficking. These plans provide a guide for what governments need to do in order to strengthen their efforts, and NGOs like World Vision with a roadmap that shows a government's priorities. These action plans create an opening to work alongside governments to accomplish their goals. For example, after continued engagement from the United Nations Special Rapporteur for Children in Armed Conflict and consistent pressure from the TIP Report, in 2012, the Myanmar Government and the Country Task Force for Monitoring and Reporting (CTFMR—of which World Vision is a member) created a Joint Action Plan to cease the recruitment and use of child soldiers in the national army. To date, 273 children have been demobilized though hundreds more suspected cases have yet to be addressed.

Once a NAP is in place, it is a vital tool that holds the implementing government accountable and shows where the successes shine and gaps remain. The National Action Plans in Cambodia, Laos, Myanmar, Philippines, and Vietnam came after recommendations from the TIP Report with additional engagement from the U.S. Embassies and the United Nations. In Myanmar, the Philippines, and Vietnam, the government has made concerted efforts to include local and international organizations into the implementation of the action plans, again in part as a result from TIP Report recommendations.

The response of governments in the region often focuses on national efforts, as opposed to implementation at the local level. Our ETIP program in the region convenes trafficking survivors who provide recommendations to government officials on such things as how to get quick access to identification documents for survivors returning from abroad. While these conversations influence discussions within the capital, slower implementation due to lack of local government awareness, capacity, and funding often hinders the effectiveness of the changes that come about. Yet awareness at the local level is starting to grow as a direct result of findings from the TIP Report and State Department engagement. Myanmar has made strong efforts to increase awareness of human trafficking across the country. These efforts include a National Anti-Trafficking Day; partnering with MTV Exit and other partners to host concerts and informational events for young people; setting up billboards with hotline numbers; broadcasting and publishing public service announcements on TV, radio, and daily newspapers, and expanding the government's Anti-Trafficking Division to start reaching out to more rural areas. As the TIP Report points out, the Government of Myanmar still has work to do and Myanmar remains on the Tier 2 Watchlist. We are, however, seeing progress as a result of the continuing conversations generated in part through the TIP Report.

It is critical to point out that governments cannot make progress alone. There is no single intervention or effort that alone can defeat the use of forced labor and human trafficking in the long term. World Vision programs are most successful when we take a multifaceted, multisector approach to combating exploitation.

Often times, the most effective efforts seemingly have nothing to do with forced labor but in fact are aimed at strengthening the formal (governmental) and informal (community-based) systems of protection that form a complete safety net for parents and children. For example, World Vision implements the Cambodians EXCEL (Eliminating eXploitive Child Labor through Education and Livelihoods). Funded by the U.S. Department of Labor, Cambodians EXCEL reaches 28,000 children working in fishing, agriculture, domestic servitude, and other sectors. Child labor in Cambodia results from factors like poverty, lack of access to quality education, cultural acceptance of child labor, debt, migration, and lack of regulation in the informal sector, particularly in subsistence farming and fishing. The program aims to remove kids from dangerous or exploitative working conditions and get them back to school through tutoring and catchup classes.

The focus on education is particularly important. World Vision research found that the higher the literacy level of a child, the more aware they are of human trafficking. World Vision and our local partners then work with children's parents to increase and diversify household income and to provide safe options for saving and obtaining credit. Access to income and credit reduces the incentive to remove a child from school and send him or her to work. This also keeps families out of debt and makes them less likely to migrate to find work or place their kids into a risky situations. A World Vision project in the Philippines—a model for the Cambodian project and also funded by U.S. Department of Labor—uses a similar approach that has removed over 70,000 children out of the worst forms of child labor or prevented them from even being subjected to this labor.

World Vision also focuses on another key factor that most people take for granted: birth registration. Human traffickers pursue individuals who are vulnerable and powerless. Without a birth certificate, children are an especially easy target.

According to UNICEF, every year 51 million children are never registered at birth, leaving them without an official name or nationality. There are an estimated 135 million unregistered children in East Asia alone. Children without a birth certificate are denied basic opportunities and their lives read like a checklist to human traffickers: poor, no education, unable to access safe credit, separated from family with no identification, and unable to verify their age. Lack of age verification makes forced marriage easier.

Birth registration impacts all aspects of a child's well-being. A birth certificate helps protect children from human trafficking, child labor, early marriage, underage recruitment, and conscription into military service. If a child is abused, neglected, exploited, or exposed to violence, a birth certificate ensures his or her access to services and justice systems. It is also critical for obtaining identity documents needed for transborder migration for work. It is therefore unsurprising to see that 80 percent of children in Vietnam, which has almost universal birth registration at 99 percent, are more aware of the need to travel with identity documents. By comparison, only 60 percent of children in Burma, which has an 81-percent registration rate, have such awareness. WV is partnering with Plan International and the U.N. in organizing the Ministerial Conference on Civil Registration and Vital Statistics (CRVS) in the Asia and Pacific in November 2014. This is an opportunity to raise awareness and generate governmental action on what is the foundation for the protection and well-being of children.

The U.S. Government has multiple options for partnering with East Asian governments and civil societies to strengthen the overall response to these crimes and prevent them from happening in the first place. In addition to the diplomatic tool of the TIP Report, the U.S. Government has tools to build on the recommendations of the TIP Report with strategic, bilateral partnerships in focus countries. For instance, the Trafficking Victims Protection Act of 2013 included the key provisions of the Child Protection Compact Act (CPCA). This allows the State Department to partner with a government and set measurable goals over a multiyear period to strengthen the protection system for vulnerable children and improve justice systems so they investigate and prosecute those who would exploit a child. This is an exciting opportunity for sustained engagement of the U.S. Government on these issues and we're looking forward to the State Department launching this effort.

Another opportunity lies with the U.S. Agency for International Development (USAID). In 2012, USAID unveiled the agency's Counter Trafficking in Persons (CTIP) Policy. In 2013, they released a field guide for USAID missions to assist in the implementation of the policy. One of the programming objectives calls for AID to begin integrating CTIP efforts into larger programming sectors such as agriculture, health, economic growth, education, and humanitarian assistance. This will allow for an increase in anti-trafficking efforts that take the multifaceted approach

42

that is proving effective at targeting the root causes of vulnerability. Furthermore, another programming objective of the CTIP policy is specific CTIP investments in what AID calls ''Critical TIP Challenge Countries.'' These are countries that have global strategic importance yet have significant trafficking problems. Of particular focus are countries that have spent several years on the Tier 2 Watchlist or Tier 3 of the TIP Report. This creates opportunities for impactful engagement with several countries in East Asia.

Finally, further opportunities exist in the Action Plan for Children in Adversity (APCA). Launched in 2012, the Action Plan unites and aligns 30 offices in seven U.S. Government agencies around the same measurable, achievable goals for international programs relating to vulnerable children. The three main objectives are strong beginnings (ensuring children meet early childhood development milestones), family care first (making sure every child is in a safe family environment), and stronger prevention and response to violence, abuse, neglect, and exploitation. The Action Plan, currently coordinated by USAID, enables U.S. Government agencies to coordinate their efforts to make U.S. programs more effective and efficient. The selection of the first focus countries will provide an opportunity to show how coordinated and multifaceted programs can collectively contribute to reducing the vulnerability of children.

These tools allow for constructive and coordinated bilateral engagement that will enable countries to develop and expand the systems of prevention, protection, and prosecution, and ideally address many of the root causes of trafficking in the region. With the right engagement and approaches, we can mitigate trafficking and eliminate it as much as it possible.

Recommendations:

• Encourage the administration to use bilateral tools like the Action Plan for Children in Adversity and Child Protection Compact Act that foster collaboration, sustainably strengthening systems, and measurable results.
• Support current U.S. Government birth registration efforts by introducing and passing the Girls Count Act in the Senate and urge the U.S. Government to support the implementation of East Asia Ministerial Plan of Action (2015–2024) that will be finalized during the Ministerial Conference in November 2014.
• Encourage USAID to further roll out their Counter-Trafficking in Persons (CTIP) policy which calls for integrating anti-trafficking efforts into other programs like economic development, emergency response, health, and education, and other steps and makes augmented investments in TIP Challenge Countries.

Congress has given the administration good tools. It is critical that we work together so these tools are used and not left to rust in the toolbox. Thank you again for holding this hearing and for all the work you continue to do in the fight against forced labor and human trafficking. World Vision is committed to working with the subcommittee on these critical issues and I look forward to answering your questions.

Senator CARDIN. Well, again, I thank both of you for your advocacy in this area.

I want to touch on the two areas that we need to have a better public understanding of what is going on. I know very well that we had real problems with trafficking for prostitution, and convincing the public that the people being trafficked were victims. And it took a major effort to be able to turn that around. And I think we have, today, and I think that most people, globally, understand that those who are trafficked for sex are victims, and are now being treated as victims. Took a long time for law enforcement to understand that these people are victims.

Now, with labor trafficking, it is even more difficult, because I do not think people really understand that there are people being trafficked and sold to a boat for 9 years for fishing. I do not think they really understand. We have up to 4 million people in Malaysia that are emigrants. Now, I am not saying all of them are being handled illegally or trafficked, but there is a large number, and we do not see the faces.

Can you explain to us how these companies operate in regards to debt bondage and can you just give us a typical example, a person who is trying to seek a better economic life for herself or himself, gets trapped with the traffickers and gets caught in debt bondage.

Ms. MISRA. Thank you for the question, Senator Cardin.

So, in the East Asian countries—and I worked in Indonesia for several years, so I saw this firsthand myself—the way it happens is that usually companies in every industry, from the formal economy to the informal economy, factories, agriculture, construction, domestic work, et cetera, hire these employment agencies to find cheap labor for them in some of the poorer countries in the region—Indonesia, Nepal, Cambodia, Burma, et cetera. And these companies will have agents—sometimes they are independent agents, sometimes they work directly for the company—who will go into the villages to recruit workers. And what we find is a lot of false promises being made about the terms and conditions of work, the wages, and then also fees being charged directly to the workers for every aspect of the recruitment process, from getting their passport to just paying the recruiter for helping them to look for a job. And if these costs were minimal, then maybe they would be justifiable, but we have seen cases of people paying 5,000 U.S. dollars, 20,000, 30,000, just for the privilege of being able to labor for somebody else. And, as a labor rights activist, we find it very hard to accept that the definition of ''work'' is being redefined as ''I pay you for the privilege of laboring for you.''

Then once these recruiters find the workers—and the workers obviously do not have this money to pay up front—they either take loans directly from the labor recruiters or from loan sharks in their villages or even, in some countries, from official government banks that charge high interest rates, or sometimes their wages are directly deducted—in collusion with the employer—from their paychecks, so they actually do not see any wages for months to pay back these recruitment fees.

And then, once they get to the country of destination, into the job that they were promised—again, oftentimes these jobs are very different than what they were promised, they are not paid the wages that they were promised, and we see conditions of forced labor. And here is where the debt bondage comes in. Because these workers often come in with visas tied to a particular employer, if they are being exploited or abused by that employer, the debt that they have keeps them in that job, because they cannot move because of the conditions of their visa to another job.

The other thing that we see in terms of debt bondage is complicity of government officials, where government officials actually take kickbacks, threaten the workers if they do not pay back the debts; or, in certain countries, like Vietnam, we actually see government officials running these recruitment agencies and making money out of it.

A good example of government complicity in labor recruitment violations is in Cambodia. Cambodia has a new section in their interior ministry to deal with labor migration. The person that they nominated to put in that position, his sister, runs one of the largest labor recruitment agencies in Cambodia and that agency has actually been found to traffic domestic workers to Malaysia. And yet, he is running the Division of the Interior Ministry in Cambodia.

And so, there are lots of issues involved with that bondage, but that is the traditional way that we see it.

Senator CARDIN. Mr. Eaves, the fishing industry is notorious for laboring. Can you just give us an idea of how that recruitment works, for the fishing boats?

Mr. EAVES. Yes. In fact, what we often see is people from the poorer countries in the region—Burma, Cambodia, Vietnam, Laos—because the demand is so high for unskilled labor, and it is actually so easy to cross the border, very often they will be recruited in their home country or will hear that there are jobs available on fishing boats. Sometimes, as was the case in Min Min, the boy that we highlighted in our testimony, he thought he was coming just to work on the docks, and it was not until he showed up that a man who told him he was going to get him the job sold him to an Indonesian fishing vessel.

And because these ships are so often at sea for so long, it is very hard to regulate. They are in international waters. And once someone is on those ships, the litany of abuses that happens to them is absolutely terrifying, and you hear about people being thrown overboard, being tortured, being killed for trying to escape. Min Min actually was able to slip out when they got close to land, and found himself in Indonesia, but he did not have any documents, he had nothing to prove who he was. And it was only after some local village people helped him contact the World Vision office in Burma, which then got in touch with the Burmese Government and helped get him back. So often—I mean, he was definitely lucky. He was one in the minority that are able to escape that.

So, that is not to say that not every fishing boat that is operating in the Andaman Sea or elsewhere is full of exploitation, but we do see a high number of people being recruited to the fishing industry.

Senator CARDIN. The three areas of recommendations that you made—the trade agreements, dealing with legislation to deal with labor recruiters, and then more consumer activism—consumers understanding what they are involved with—I wanted to concentrate on the third point for one moment.

Could you elaborate more how you could map the supply chain so that consumers would have better information as to where products are being produced as it relates to forced labor?

Ms. MISRA. Thank you, Senator Cardin.

I think that the responsibility for mapping the supply chain needs to be put on companies and employers, particularly the end buyers of this. Jesse and I are both members of a coalition called the Alliance to End Slavery and Trafficking, ATEST, and we have engaged with a number of employers on this issue who often make arguments that their supply chain is so long, it is difficult to map. However, the Solidarity Center has mapped the supply chain of shrimp from Thailand to grocery stores here in the United States. The Guardian just did it recently with the fishing boat story and was able to tie it directly to grocery stories both in the United States and abroad. So, we think that it is not as difficult as they say it is, and that there should be an affirmative responsibility for them to do that.

So, that is the first step in the process. I mean, I think it is very difficult for a consumer to be able to figure out where their shrimp or their garments are coming from.

With that said, there are different opportunities now, because of the Internet, because of different apps, such as FreeToWork, Slave-Free—what is the SlaveFree—there is another app—SlaveFree-Footprint, et cetera, that consumers can find out more information. The companies are given grades on what they are doing to address forced labor problems, et cetera. But, we really believe that it should be the responsibility of the companies, and that they can do it. And one way to do that is through economic pressure, which we can talk about later.

Senator CARDIN. Thank you.

Senator Rubio.

Senator RUBIO. Thank you, Mr. Chairman.

Ms. Misra, I wanted to ask you about labor recruiters. You touched upon that in your statement earlier. They often, you know, promise victims these lucrative jobs, and then they force them to work in either forced labor or prostitution. So, if you could elaborate a little bit more on the type of prevention programs that exist in some of these countries that prevent people from falling into these false promises. In essence, what I am looking for is examples of programs that are actually working or are successful at making headway and making people less vulnerable to these recruiters.

Ms. MISRA. Thank you, Senator Rubio.

And actually, one of the things that we are looking for also is good practices in this area, which is very difficult to find in the labor recruitment process.

A few things that we have seen that have worked, first of all, is the elimination, completely, of recruitment fees. Anytime that a country allows recruitment fees, it ends up being abused, and people end up in situations of debt bondage. So, really the first thing is to promote ''no fees.'' And we have seen that in certain sectors. We have not seen it across the board in any of the countries in East Asia, elimination of recruitment fees. But, we have seen it in certain sections or for—when certain employers mandate it, and then the recruiters that recruit for them do that.

I will say this is one of the areas—why I mentioned earlier that we would like to see the U.S. Government take a lead on this. Already, the Congress and the President, through the NDAA, in the Executive order last year, have eliminated fees and regulated labor recruiters further for government procurement processes. And then, as I mentioned—I cannot say thank you enough to you about this—but, in S. 744, Subtitle F removes those recruitment fees. And we think that that is going to set a great precedent for the rest of the world that we will be able to use.

The last thing that I will just say on this is, the ILO just negotiated this past June a new supplement to the 1930 Forced Labor Instrument Protocol. And as part of it—and I was part of these negotiations—it calls for the elimination of recruitment fees, in the regulation, of labor recruiters.

Senator RUBIO. And I wanted to ask you, also, because you touched upon this a little bit, and actually, so did the chairman earlier, when he talked about some of these consumer products that, in the United States, are being bought or consumed that are, in some cases, potentially done through forced labor or child labor—what are the industries that are the most dependent on trafficked labor in Asia?

Ms. MISRA. So, seafood processing would be high on the list. The second one, I would say, is ready-made garments. We have seen a lot of issues of forced labor, debt bondage, in the ready-made garment industry, in terms of what is exported to the United States. Regionally, you know, there are a lot of issues with construction and domestic work. But, I would say, in terms of products that come into the United States, it is really ready-made garments and seafood.

Senator RUBIO. And, Mr. Eaves, in your testimony you list several factors that can prevent child trafficking—you know, high literacy rates, birth registration. Can you just describe a little bit more in detail how these factors prevent children from entering the trafficking cycle?

Mr. EAVES. Absolutely. I will give an example from a program that we have in the Philippines that is similar to the one we have in Cambodia, where you have a high number of children who are forced to work in the sugarcane industry and then also in the fishing industry and as forced domestic servants. What we do is, we identify children who are working, find out the circumstances of them being in that position, and then we work with their families and with the employer to get them out of that situation and back into school. But, that only does so much, because oftentimes they are there because their parents are not making enough income to be able to support their family. And so, they pull their kids out of school, will give them to a labor recruiter or let them work for very cheap, because some money is better than none.

And so, what we will then do is work with those families to do everything from working—they can have backyard gardens and communal gardens, so they can sell food for more money. They receive training on how to start a business, how to run a business, kind of, you know, Business 101; make sure that they can have access to safe lines of credit so that they are not taking out debts and placing their family in debt bondage.

So, you are looking at all the different areas that can force a family into a situation where they find themselves handing over a child or themselves to someone who does not want to do the right thing by that child. And so, we have seen—in the Philippine example—we have seen over 70,000 children removed from hazardous and exploitative child labor, and not go back in, as a result of their family having the income and the kids having access to an education and a community that has become empowered to stand up and chase people away who are trying to recruit kids.

Senator RUBIO. You touched upon the Philippines. I wanted to follow up, because I know the organization World Vision is involved there in the relief efforts in the aftermath of the huge storm that they had. I was concerned—and I visited there earlier this year—about the impact that the—anytime, we have seen in the past, like in earthquakes in Haiti, that there have been massive displacements, the signal goes off in my mind, and in the mind of many, that this creates increased vulnerability for children to be trafficked, and even adults, for that matter. What has been, in your view, perhaps—you may not be familiar with it, but perhaps you are—if you could share with us, if you do have this information—what has been the aftermath of the storm? Have we seen an increase in vulnerability and/or trafficking as a result of it? Have the authorities there been able to do a good job of keeping that from happening?

Mr. EAVES. Actually, I was just in the Philippines last month in the typhoon-affected areas. And so, one of the things that we have done is, USAID has provided funding to start a project looking at preventing and responding to vulnerability to trafficking. And the way they are doing it is through their larger counter-trafficking-in-persons policy, which they launched last year, which calls for an integration of not only addressing human trafficking, but looking at other issues, as well, integrating kind of a trafficking focus into other sectors. In this case, it is livelihoods or helping people earn a living again.

And so, we are implementing a project in Ormoc province, which was one of the most heavily damaged and where we have seen most of—you know, most of the children have not been able to return to school, there is high levels of vulnerability, people's entire crops and livelihoods have been wiped out. And so, we know of cases where children have been trafficked.

And adults, in particular, are incredibly susceptible to labor recruiters, under the circumstances that Neha was talking about. And so, as part of this project, we are working with these families to be able to earn an income so they can protect themselves while at the same time educating them on the dangers of labor recruiters and risky migration practices, and trying to keep them in their home communities, where they can try to get their lives back on track and rebuild after the storm.

But, that is an example of how the U.S. Government can engage from multiple angles to prevent vulnerability to trafficking while also improving people's income and safety at the same time.

Senator RUBIO. Thank you.

Senator CARDIN. Let me thank both of you for your testimony.

Ms. Misra, if you will follow up with us on the mapping issue, the corporate responsibility, company responsibility, I would appreciate that, because I think we are all interested.

And I think most people in this country—a large number of people in this country would not want to participate in forced labor. So, given the opportunity, I think they would take action. So, I would be interested as to how you see reasonable, responsible regulations or laws that could help consumers be better consumers in this area. So, if you could make that available to us, I would very much appreciate it.

Senator CARDIN. And we thank both of you for your testimony. This, to me, has been a very helpful hearing. As I said in the opening, it is a dimension of our Rebalance to Asia that needs to have a spotlight on it, and I think this hearing has helped us do that. And I thank you both for your participation.

Ms. MISRA. Thank you very much.

Mr. EAVES. Thank you.

Senator CARDIN. With that, we will keep the record open until the close of business on Thursday.

And the subcommittee stands adjourned.

[Whereupon, at 11:55 a.m., the hearing was adjourned.]